SEAFARERS' VOICES 3

Slaver Captain

SLAVER CAPTAIN

John Newton

Edited with an introduction by
Vincent McInerney

Seaforth
PUBLISHING

This edition copyright © A Vincent McInerney 2010

First published in Great Britain in 2010 by
Seaforth Publishing,
Pen & Sword Books Ltd,
47 Church Street,
Barnsley S70 2AS

www.seaforthpublishing.com

British Library Cataloguing in Publication Data
A catalogue record for this book is available
from the British Library
ISBN 978 1 84832 079 6

Typeset and designed by M.A.T.S. Leigh-on-Sea, Essex
Printed and bound in Great Britain by
CPI Antony Rowe, Chippenham, Wiltshire

Contents

Contents

Contents

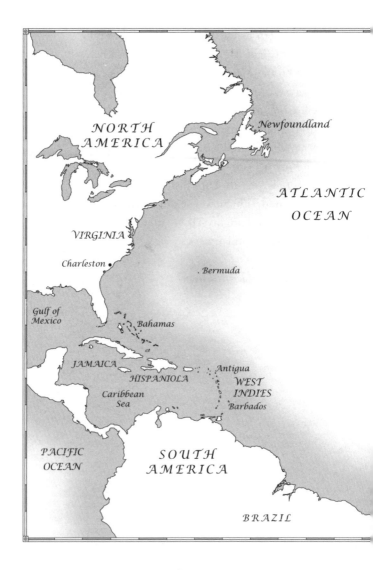

Isle of Lewis

Lough Swilly

Londonderry

SCOTLAND

GREAT
BRITAIN

IRELAND Liverpool

Harwich

London

NETHERLANDS

Bristol

Plymouth Maidstone

Portsmouth

EUROPE

FRANCE

SPAIN

PORTUGAL

Azores

Madeira

Canaries

AFRICA

Cape Verde
Islands

Cape
Verde

SENEGAMBIA

R. Gambia

Rio Grande

Benanoes

SIERRA

Plantanes

LEONE

Sherbro Island

Cape Mount

Windward
Coast

Bight of
Benin

Cape Palmas

Gold Coast

Bight of
Biafra

Cape Lopez

ANGOLA

Editorial Note

THERE CAN BE HARDLY be a moment, day or night, when the hymn 'Amazing Grace' is not being sung, played, or thought about somewhere on Earth. What many will not know is the history of the author of the verses that were eventually to become that hymn – John Newton (1725-1807). Newton's account of his life, and of his thoughts in maturity of his participation in the African slave trade, are the subject of the third in the Seafarers' Voices series, to follow the autobiographies of the galley slave, Jean Marteilhe (1684-1770) and the privateer, George Shelvocke (1675-1742).

But even those who know the name of John Newton, and his relationship with 'Amazing Grace', may hardly be aware of the many twists and turns in the long road of his life. We hear of his obsessive love for the young Mary Catlett, daughter of a distant relation; his desertion from the Royal Navy to spend time with Mary; his recapture and public flogging on HMS *Harwich*, followed by his exchange into a Guineaman, a ship trading along the African coasts. He became effectively a slave of another trader in Africa, then made the transition to become a slaver himself. He made first one trip as mate of the *Brownlow* (1748-49), then three as captain (1749-54), of first the *Duke of Argyle*, then the *African*, sailing out of Liverpool, Britain's premier slaving port in the late eighteenth century. After being forced to retire from slaving through illness, Newton was eventually, after many setbacks and refusals, ordained into the Church of England ministry, ending his life as a fashionable London preacher, and confidant and adviser of such politicians as the slave trade abolitionist, William Wilberforce (1759-1833).

This third volume of Seafarers' Voices has been chosen because it deals with an issue that still reverberates down the years, and the consequences of which we still live with today: the brutal human trade in indigenous Africans and their transport as slaves for sale in the West Indian and American markets. The account is of further interest because it comes from one who was heavily involved in this trade for four years, but who also knew it from both sides, himself having been a captive in all but name in Sierra Leone.

The present volume will comprise two separate accounts written by Newton and brought together to try to give an overall picture of Newton and the driving forces which shaped his thinking and career. *Thoughts on the African Slave Trade* (1788) was written when abolition was already an unstoppable *cause célèbre*, and Newton finally felt impelled to confess to the part he played in the trade, and plead the cause of abolition. Newton's memoirs, *An Authentic Narrative* (1764), consist of a series of fourteen letters sent to the Reverend Thomas Haweis, at Haweis' suggestion, to try to facilitate Newton's entry into the Anglican ministry. These letters deal with Newton's spiritual conversion to Christianity, a form of *Bildungsroman* of the soul, where the account of Newton's career as a seafarer and slaving captain is subsidiary to his spiritual journey. As neither of these volumes separately seem to reveal the man behind the face, bringing together the two as one make it possible to present an overall picture of this – for all his seeming approachability – elusive character.

The editions used are the third of *An Authentic Narrative* (1765) and the first of *Thoughts* (1788). Texts have been reduced from an overall count of 41,000 words to 33,000. Losses of text are through repetition, theological argument, and observations of perhaps limited interest to those interested primarily in maritime aspects of the work. Spelling, punctuation and syntax have been moderated to meet modern expectations.

Introduction

> Beware the Bight of Benin!
> Beware the Bight of Benin!
> For every *four* that come out,
> *Seven* sailors go in!
> Street skipping song from Liverpool

THE MEMOIRS OF AN eighteenth-century clergyman might at first sight seem an odd choice for a volume within the series of Seafarers' Voices, yet the life of the Reverend John Newton, who ended his days respectably as the Rector of St Mary Woolnoth in London at the ripe old age of 82, is a tale that began with seafaring and adventure and involved not a few skirmishes with death. It is also a tale of mutiny, impressment, desertion, and the brutality of the African slave trade. Narratives such as Newton's accounts of his involvement in the slave trade are rare: part of the uniqueness of this text is that it was written by a trader himself, a man with first-hand experience of this most terrible trade, and it is distinguished by its detailed and vivid evocation of the implicit horror and danger inherent in the life of a slaver captain.

Newton's story is not well-known in the history of

seafaring, and it is one which should not go unread. By his own account it is a tale of brinkmanship in a series of escapades which involved a cliffhanger existence of being repeatedly delivered from threats and danger, and at the last possible moment finding himself retrieved from impending doom. His adventures at sea were spent both as officer and plain sailor; not only did he end his seafaring life as the captain of an African slave trader plying the Middle Passage between the Windward Coast and the West Indies, he also spent time as a captive himself, the prisoner of an African princess, as well as a period of 'going native', when he was settled on the African coast to the point of being unwilling to come home to England.

The two memoirs which make up this third volume of the series of Seafarers' Voices are *Thoughts on the African Slave Trade: A Memoir of my Infidel Days as a Slaving Captain* (1788) and *An Authentic Narrative of Some Remarkable Particulars in the Life of John Newton* (1764). *Thoughts on the African Slave Trade* was written as a contribution to contemporary debates on the abolitionist cause, and is distinguished not only by the eloquence of its argument, but also by the sympathetic tone which encourages the reader to feel empathy with the enslaved Africans as fellow human beings; at the same time it provides an explicit account of the human cruelty and brutality which characterised that trade. This piece was written as a 'confession' of

Newton's personal involvement in the horrors of the trade, and in support of the movement for abolition of the slave trade, and pulls no punches in its descriptions. Although the *Thoughts* were written after the *Authentic Narrative*, they have been placed first in this volume as they present the more vivid account of the seafaring part of Newton's career, and make explicit what is only implicit in the memoirs contained in his *Authentic Narrative*.

Authentic that narrative may be, but at its heart is a resounding silence regarding the horrific reality of the human trade by which Newton had earned a living before abandoning the seafaring life for health reasons. The *Authentic Narrative* was originally written as a series of letters to the Reverend Thomas Haweis, a curriculum vitae for Newton as a man eager to be accepted as a clergyman in the Church of England, but who was being held back by a lack of a university education and appropriate connections, besides suffering from non-clerical, Nonconformist origins. To that end the *Authentic Narrative* is a narrative of spiritual growth, a story of a 'brand plucked out of the burning fire', or from a modern perspective, a tale of a rebellious and troublesome teenager who eventually made good.

The story of the life of John Newton, variously sailor, captive, slaver captain, anti-slavery campaigner and writer of the hymn 'Amazing Grace', still resonates today. Newton's life has featured in two recent films,

Amazing Grace (2006), in which Newton was played by Albert Finney, and *The Amazing Grace* (2006), starring Nick Moran, not to mention the play *African Snow* which was performed in London's West End in 2007 (a snow was a smallish, two-masted, square-rigged vessel of around 150 tons, on which Newton voyaged from Liverpool to Africa). His role on both sides of the slave trade is mentioned in countless histories of the slave trade and the campaigns to abolish it, and he was adviser to William Wilberforce (1759-1853), English politician and leader of the campaign to abolish the trade. He also remains a revered character for Evangelical Christians, not only for his preaching and his life as a clergyman, but also for the dramatic nature of his spiritual journey and conversion to Christianity, from the depths of the self-confessed sinfulness of his maritime life to his eventual ordination as a clergyman in the Church of England, in spite of the social and educational barriers he faced.

John Newton's life started quietly enough: he was born in Wapping in 1725, in the heart of the London docklands by the river Thames. His father was a merchant sea captain – an austere and distant man who was often away at sea – and his mother educated him at home until her early death when John was only seven years old. Apparently his mother hoped that Newton would eventually become a minister of religion, but she was a practising Nonconformist, and this religious and social background would not have recommended him to the Church of England when his spiritual vocation arose later in life. After her death, Newton was educated at boarding school for a couple of years, but he went to sea for the first time with his father at around the age of ten or eleven, and at that point his formal education ended. Beyond that point he was entirely self-educated, much of which education took place on the sea voyages he made as a slaver captain. He also, bizarrely enough, engaged in the study of Euclidean mathematics during his sufferings as a slave in all but name in the Plantain Islands off the west coast of Africa, using a stick for a pen and a sandy beach for paper.

In the *Authentic Narrative*, Newton writes about the spiritual nature of his voyaging, the oceans being a place where battles with the elements and storms at sea are the backdrop for his headlong descent into sin and wretchedness, only for him to experience a spiritual reawakening in the face of potential shipwreck and death. This closeness to the elements and closeness to mortality provoke in him a looking inward, and a deep philosophical and spiritual engagement. Biblical rhythms and images imbue his language, as he tells us his tale of his repeated challenges to authority and his deliberate adoption of behaviours calculated to make him deeply unpopular with the captains under whom he served. Although Newton's father was not especially well-connected in social or naval terms, he had enough influence and friends to ensure that, when impressed, Newton was able to serve as midshipman, rather than ordinary sailor. His father was able to secure him other work on ships captained by acquaintances. But even with these advantages, Newton managed by his rebellious and challenging attitudes to get himself demoted below decks, whipped for desertion, and generally made himself *persona non grata*.

Newton is much more matter of fact when talking of the events of his life at sea than he is when he uses dramatic and apocalyptic imagery in, for example, the description of his prophetic Venetian dream. He does not dwell on the fine detail of his public flogging, nor the details of life on board ship, in spite of the fact that as a captain he kept detailed logs of weather, position, route, supplies, and all the day-to-day minutiae so crucial to his business at sea.[1] However, when he speaks of embarking on a potential five-year voyage after his impressment, desertion and demotion, he captures vividly the powerlessness and misery of the pressed sailor as he sets off over the oceans away from familiar shores, not knowing if or when he will return. That Newton had a gift for language we can see not only from his writing, but also from his description of writing a song which ridiculed the captain on one voyage, a song which he managed to teach to the whole ship's crew. Perhaps also his eloquence was twinned with charm: in spite of his self-confessed bad behaviour he managed to persuade some lieutenants whom 'he had used ill' to allow him to escape from that five-year voyage by exchanging onto another ship, or perhaps they were eager to grasp a chance to rid themselves of a troublemaker with a wicked tongue.

In the *Authentic Narrative*, Newton tells us much of his misadventures on the west coast of Africa. He ended up as the prisoner of an African 'princess' named PI, the wife of a European slave trader. This time in Africa was a period of being brought low, of living in abject poverty and near-slavery, suffering from starvation, and being an object of pity to African slaves. Later in life this experience seems to have given him an insight and sympathy with the plight of the slave, which emerges in *Thoughts on the African Slave Trade*, but this empathy was some time in coming, for he very soon ended up on the other side of the trade himself. In spite of his trials when under the power of the bullying PI, this descent into the depths of suffering was not the impetus for his religious conversion: when he found an avenue of escape from this servitude he ended up working for a slave dealer. Several biographers speculate that Newton, as he puts it, became 'a white man grown black', and possibly even took an African mistress or dabbled in local spiritual beliefs, as he became thoroughly absorbed in the life and trade of the Windward Coast of Africa.

However, thanks to his father's maritime connections

and friendship with one of the most prominent Liverpool merchants involved in the slave trade, Joseph Manesty, Newton was eventually rescued, albeit unwillingly, and taken home. His contentment with and integration into life on the Windward Coast is indicated by the fact that he had to be persuaded back home by tales of a substantial inheritance (which proved untrue), but his continuing attachment to a girl named Mary Catlett, who was the daughter of old friends of his mother and who eventually became his wife, was the overriding factor which drew him back to England.

Newton dismisses his voyage home as 'tedious' to recount, yet it was also the scene of 'the most horrid impiety and profaneness', drunkenness and blasphemy. Once again we are led to feel that Newton was a most dangerous person to know: over and again in his account his companions in sin meet their ends by shipwreck or drowning, while Newton sees himself as singled out, a special example of the depths of sinfulness to which man can descend, but preserved for a special purpose. This voyage, which nearly ended in shipwreck after the most violent of storms, was the scene of Newton's spiritual transformation and new-found acceptance of the Christian message, and here his eloquence in recounting his emergence from sin into faith enabled him to reach his goal of ordination. Thomas Haweis showed Newton's letters to the influential Lord Dartmouth, who persuaded the Bishop of

Lincoln to ordain Newton into the Church of England in April 1762: Newton was given the post of curate-in-charge at Olney in Buckinghamshire. Lord Dartmouth then funded the publishing of the letters as the *Authentic Narrative*; the publication was a success, and the transformation from rough sailor to religious gentleman was complete. Newton's new career as a clergyman prominent in the Evangelical Christian movement was well on its way.[2]

It was not until 1788, over thirty years after his last voyage as captain of a slave ship, that Newton published *Thoughts on the African Slave Trade*, at the beginning of which he admits that it was not only intended as a contribution to the arguments for the abolition of the slave trade, but also as 'a public confession' of his former active involvement in that trade. This piece is carefully constructed and argued, the arguments are set out methodically, and Newton appeals both to national self-interest and common humanity in the way that he depicts the slave trade as equally harmful to all those involved. He is quick to claim that he is pleading this cause to vindicate the wrongs of the oppressed from a religious, rather than a political standpoint; he explicitly states that this trade is 'always unjustifiable', but that inattention and self-interest prevented this fact being perceived. The effect, he claimed, is to efface all moral sensibility. In this we see a striving to account for the inherent tension and contradiction between the intensity of his spiritual and religious study and introspection during his voyages as first mate, then captain on slaver ships, a spiritual journey which he described so fully in the *Authentic Narrative*, at the same time that he was 'an accessory to misery' and 'an active instrument' in the brutal trade he describes in *Thoughts*.

Newton eventually gave up the slave trade, not because of moral qualms at the time, but for the sake of his health. He considered it essentially 'a genteel employment', that is, sanctioned by the norms of middle-class society, but personally he felt that he was no more than a 'gaoler or turnkey'. Yet the health problem which caused him to cease this employment was a sudden fit, two days before sailing from Liverpool once more as captain of a slave trader. This seizure rendered him unconscious, and left him 'such a pain and dizziness in my head', that medical advice warned that it would be unsafe to undertake the voyage. Newton lived, as we have seen, on into his eighties, so whatever caused this fit did not persist: perhaps the fit was a response to the horror of the voyage he was about to embark upon. He lost consciousness, and woke up to find his old life closed to him. However, another, better, life offered itself, and he was eventually able to find himself new employment, and a new, suitably genteel, identity as Tide Surveyor, in charge of the customs office at Liverpool.

However, the slaves who had joined his slave ship had already lost their homes and become detached from their origins when he took them on board his slave ship; their new lives only promised brutality and misery, and once in Captain Newton's care they lost their former identities, too. As slaves began to arrive they were entered in Newton's journal as numbers; they had now become commodities, mere cargo:

No 4	A fine man bought from Mr Langton (a black trader).
No 22	One boy, four foot.
No 24-26	Three girls, undersize.
No 28	A man, brought by Mr Bridson (1st Mate).
No 31	A small girl, three foot.[3]

Once purchased, slaves would be branded with the initials of their owners with a red-hot iron: on Newton's ship it would be 'JM' for Joseph Manesty,[4] his father's friend, his patron, and the Liverpool merchant funding and bearing the risk of the voyage. Slaves arriving on board could also be refused, exchanged, or resold to other captains, and Newton's journal mentions exchanging a variety of boys and girls with one Captain Williams, the latter seeking 'only for small slaves'. The turning of humanity into commodity was complete.

In *Thoughts* we find explicit and harrowing descriptions of the horrors of the conditions on slave ships, the brutality of the treatment meted out to the slaves, and the way that this trade truly debased *all* of the participants. In this account, Newton is distinctive among his contemporaries in the way that he denies the slaves as 'other' or 'savage' – he stressed the similarity of Europeans and Africans as human beings, and encouraged readers to exchange places with the slaves in their imagination, for example, in his emphasis on the 'modesty' of the African women, 'which would not disgrace an English woman'. However, all that Newton tells us of the way that he personally dealt with his human cargo is that he 'treat[ed] the slaves I had taken with as much humanity as a regard to my own safety would admit.' For his own safety, a captain on one of these slave ships had continually to assert his authority in the face of constant challenges and threats to that authority. A crowded, disease-ridden slave ship which might have to cruise the slave coast for months, as it gradually filled its hold with slaves, was not a place for the timid or unassertive captain. Mutinies amongst both slaves and sailors were not uncommon, and certainly, besides dealing with slave insurrections, the crew also had to be kept in order. Punishments were swift – irons or a smart dozen with the lash – but with the possibility of trouble at sea, leeway was necessary towards the crew, as at any time the slaves might somehow break free, mutiny, take the ship and murder the crew. The slave quarters below decks were eventually filled and as numbers increased, the slaves were more and more confined below to prevent trouble, rather than being allowed up on deck for (albeit limited) fresh air and exercise. The larger, stronger and more agile slaves were shackled, wrists and ankles, one-to-one – so neither could move without the consent of the other.

With overcrowding and having to use the infamous 'tubs' (lavatory receptacles, generally overflowing or out of reach, kept in the slave quarters), fevers and fluxes raged, and slaves began to die before leaving the coast. Newton, in an attempt to cut losses, tried giving rice instead of beans, washing the quarters with vinegar, and smoking them out with tobacco and brimstone. Many slaves died through the misery and stress of the unknown. As the season drew to its end, the slaves appearing for sale would be older and weaker. The slave accommodation would also now be full, and slave health (in the shape of profits) in such cramped quarters became a strong consideration. Also, early arriving ships with healthy slaves would achieve the best prices in the markets on the other side of the Atlantic. There was also the risk of tornadoes at the beginning of the stormy season, but ultimately the voyage had to be calculated on getting as many slaves as possible to market in good health. To add to the risks of the voyage, ships for the African trade were not particularly well made, and would often last for barely half a dozen voyages. There is evidence that Newton's patron, Liverpool merchant Joseph Manesty, 'sacrificed safety and durability for immediate profit'. He encouraged his Rhode Island boatbuilders to economise on construction methods, saying that 'as insurance is very high I would have as little money laid out on the vessels as possible.' The ships fell prey to the extremes of climate to which they were exposed, their joints being stressed due to the expansion and contraction of their timbers.[5]

What is also shocking to modern readers is the ubiquity of the slave trade, and the sheer numbers of people involved. As James Walvin puts it, the 'significance of the Atlantic slave trade lies not simply in the story of Africa, nor in that of the enslaved Americas, but in the way Western Europe rose to unprecedented power and material well-being on the back of the Atlantic slave system.'[6] Walvin also points to the unimaginably huge numbers involved: he states that over the course of the slave trade, around 12 million Africans survived the journey to the slave coast (it is unknown how many died along the route from the interior to the sea), and that 1.5 million died on the sea crossing. The British shipped around 3.4 million Africans from 1700 to 1810 alone.[7] These vast migrations had far-reaching consequences for the societies involved, both in human and economic terms, the long-term ramifications of which we continue to experience today. At the time of Newton's involvement, the trade was in a process of great expansion, and the political and social imbalances in the destination countries were quite astonishing; for example, in 1740 in Jamaica there were 100,000 slaves and 10,000 Europeans – the number of slaves would be double this by 1776.[8]

English slave-taking proper in Africa is considered to have begun with John Hawkins (1532-1595) who, in 1562, took three hundred Africans across to the West Indies where they were sold to Spanish planters, thus initiating the 'triangular trade', that is, from Britain to Africa with goods such as textiles, metals, hardware, spirits (especially cheap brandy), and guns, which were exchanged for slaves. The slave ships then sailed from Africa to the West Indies or Americas to sell the slaves and, if they could, stock up with cargo (sugar, coffee, rice, cotton, rum)[9] – then back to England to sell the cargo, with a potential for profit on all three legs of the voyage. Hawkins was eventually knighted by one of his slaving co-partners, Elizabeth I, and part of Hawkins' original coat of arms showed a bound black slave. Just over a hundred years later Charles II (1630-1685), perennially short of money, sold some merchants the rights to be sole traders in Africa, forming what eventually became known as the Royal African Trading Company, one of the company's duties being to supply three thousand slaves yearly to British plantations in the West Indies.

Not only did the commodities available for trading

on each leg favour the triangular trade, so too did the elements, as north Atlantic currents run clockwise, and the winds also blow that way for much of the year. On the journey south from Europe to Africa, the Canary current boosted the slave traders on their way, with the North Equatorial current speeding them on to the Caribbean. The journey home to England was made on the back of the North Atlantic current and the Gulf Stream, which 'could add up to 130 miles a day' to a ship's run.[10] On the Windward Coast, the slaving season usually lasted about six months, from November to April, when the winds and seas were favourable for small boats from the ships to go ashore through the surf to buy or barter slaves from the local African chiefs. But as collecting the slaves needed to be a year-round occupation, forts and factories were built, some with trained African soldiers, to collect and hold potential slaves until the season began again, the men running these forts and factories being known as 'resident traders'. With such easy profits on view, the Royal African Company monopoly was soon under pressure, and parliament responded by allowing 'separate traders' into the arrangement, who would pay ten per cent to the Company on everything bought or sold on the coast.

Profit underpinned the motives of all involved, Newton not excepted. In his later job as tide surveyor, which was a senior position in the Liverpool custom house, where he supervised 60 employees, he earned £40 per annum, whereas when he was a slaver captain, his basic wage was £5 per month which, although only half of the sum that a captain in the Royal Navy earned, was supplemented by a share of the profits of the voyage. Slaves who were purchased for £4 to £6 per head in Africa were sold in Jamaica for between £50 and £55 each; Newton's part in this trade earned him a bonus of £257 for a fourteen month voyage, on top of his salary of £70.[11] This was at a time when a clergyman might earn £90 in a year, depending on how lucrative his living, a surveyor £137, or a solicitor £231. [12] First mates received around £4 per month, and they also could earn a bonus. This bonus was often derived from the system of 'privilege slaves', whereby senior officers might have their own allowance of slaves to be sold on their own account at auction, perhaps a dozen for the captain, and one for the first mate. Third in importance on the ship after captain and first mate, surgeons were essential to keep up the health of the slaves, as every slave who died incurred a loss to the owners. Surgeons were paid less than £1 per week, but in addition would receive 'head money': so much per head for every slave surviving the voyage to be sold at market. One surgeon received £120 for two hundred slaves, more than the captain, but in spite of these incentives, the mortality rates amongst the transported slaves ran high: on Newton's voyage on the *Brownlow* as first mate, one-third of the 220 slaves did not survive the passage. None of the crew or slaves died on Newton's final voyage as captain of the *African*, but Newton admitted that it was due to the fact that he ended up carrying less than half of the projected amount of slaves, which mitigated the usual problems associated with overcrowding.[13]

After the surgeon came the carpenter, who had to put together the boards and dividers which would comprise the living quarters of the slaves, and the barricado, a security barrier to divide the slaves from the crew, the men from the women. This had spikes running across the top and two holes through which two guns were mounted, pointing at the slaves, and a door through which only one person could pass at a time. On nearing the coast, the carpenter had to turn the great cabin into a form of shop with shelves and counters, etc., from where the ship's barter goods would be exhibited and sold to the African and European slave traders. The carpenter's was thus an important job, for which he received more in pay than the second and third mates.

On slave ships, the lives of the European crew were not held in much account. On Newton's *Duke of Argyle* voyage, six of the thirty-strong crew died of fevers. The crew were often men who could get nothing better, or who, even though the rate of sickness and death on the African coast was frighteningly high – sometimes fifty per cent – deliberately signed on because of the general laxity on board these ships in terms of the accessibility of drink and women slaves. The wages of the common sailors in the mid-eighteenth century were around 30s or £2 per month, on top of their food and lodging on board; this was significantly higher than in other trades, but of course, the risks of these voyages were also significantly higher. Many were tempted on board by a cash advance of two or three months' wages: enough to pay off debts or indulge in some wild celebrations before setting off. This advance was also a temptation to others: apparently Liverpool landlords and landladies were disposed to have sailors imprisoned for debt, whether real or imaginary, then sell them on 'to an outward bound Guineaman [slave ship] and collect his two or three months' advance wages to pay off his debt.'[14]

Different British ports constituted the centre of the slave trade at different times, starting with London in the seventeenth century, followed by Bristol, which was the premier slave-trading port by the 1730s. Many smaller ports, such as Workington, Poole, Lancaster and Lyme Regis, were also involved, and by the mid-eighteenth century, at the time of Newton's involvement, Liverpool was in the ascendant. London merchants had originally provided the greatest source of funding, but from 1750 to 1780, 'almost three-quarters of the British slave trade was financed by Liverpool merchants.'[15] It was a risky trade, and one which required a substantial capital to enter: on a successful voyage, profits could be extremely high, but the potential for loss due to mutiny, disease, shipwreck or capture by privateers was also very great. Overall, the average rate of return for investors in the slave trade in the eighteenth century was around ten per cent, two or three times that of safer investments such as government bonds or annuities, so the return was good but not excessive by contemporary standards, and of course a measure of the high risks involved.[16] Newton's employer, Joseph Manesty, was a very active trader in the mid-eighteenth century, owning over nine vessels in his own right, and taking a share in several others.[17] Unfortunately for John Newton, Manesty did not continue making profits: in 1765 he went bankrupt, and Newton, by then an impecunious clergyman, lost his life savings, which he had entrusted to Manesty's hands.[18]

However, this was no hindrance to Newton in his career: he never lacked friends and patrons, and included the poet William Cowper and politician William Wilberforce amongst his closest confidants. His active campaigning for the abolition of slavery perhaps went some way to atone for the guilt he felt at his early involvement in such a desperate business, and his credibility as a witness for the horror of the associated trade very much derived from the fact that he could speak from personal experience of the trade, but with the later-gained authority of a man of the cloth. There are undoubtedly omissions in terms of personal culpability in *Thoughts*, even as he headlines it as a personal confession, and sometimes the reader might reasonably wonder if what Newton claims to have 'heard' is based on rather more direct experience than hearsay. This is a supposition backed up by the evidence of his manuscript diaries,[19] but that is not to diminish the value of either of the following accounts as valuable and illuminating insights into the nature of the eighteenth-century slave trade, whether as slaver captain, sailor or slave.

Part I

Thoughts on the African Slave Trade:
A Memoir of my Infidel Days as a Slaving Captain

THE EFFECT UPON THE African peoples of that disgraceful branch of commerce which has long been maintained on the coast of Africa, the sole design of which has been the purchasing of our fellow-creatures in order to supply our West India islands and the American colonies, when they were ours, with slaves is now generally understood. Indeed, so much light has been thrown upon the subject by so many able pens, and so many reputable persons have already used their utmost influence for the suppression of this traffic, that it is hoped this stain on our national character will soon be wiped out.

So if I now throw my mite into the public stock of information, it is less from a conviction that such interference is necessary, than from a belief that silence would, in me, be criminal. Even if my testimony should not be considered necessary, I still feel bound to take shame upon myself by a public confession – although it now comes far too late to repair the misery to which I have been an accessory. I hope it will always be a subject of humiliating reflection to me that I was once an active instrument in a business at which my heart now shudders – that of the slave trade.

In my youth, a series of headstrong passions and follies plunged me into a succession of difficulties and hardships, which, eventually, reduced me to seek refuge among the natives of Africa. There, for about eighteen months, I was, in effect, a captive and a slave myself, depressed to the lowest degree of wretchedness. Possibly I should not have been so completely miserable had I lived solely among the natives, but it was my lot to reside with white men of my own colour and language, persons who were settled upon that part of the Windward Coast which lies between Sierra Leone and Cape Mount for the purpose of purchasing and collecting slaves, to sell to the vessels arriving from Europe. Usually, this part of the coast proves that 'country from whose bourn / No traveller returns', to those who venture upon a temporary residence there, but the good Providence of God, without my expectation, and almost against my will, delivered me from those scenes of wickedness and woe, and I arrived at Liverpool in May 1748. However, I soon revisited the place of my captivity, as mate of a slaving vessel, and then, in the year 1750, was appointed commander of a slave ship. In this capacity I made a further three voyages to the Windward Coast for slaves, until forced into retirement from the trade by illness. In all, I first saw the coast of Guinea in the year 1745, and took my last leave of it in 1754.

This, obviously, was not an intentional farewell, but through the mercy of God it proved so. For after three voyages I had fitted out for a fourth, and was upon the point of sailing, when I was taken by a sudden illness and had to resign the ship to another captain, thus being unexpectedly freed from this disagreeable service. Disagreeable I had long found it, and I think I should have quitted it sooner had I considered it, as I now do, to be unlawful and wrong. But at that time I had never a scruple about this trade, nor was such a thought once suggested to me by any friend. What I did, I did ignorantly, considering it as the course of life which Divine Providence had allotted me, and having no concern in point of conscience but to treat the slaves I had taken with as much humanity as a regard to my own safety would admit.

The experience and observation of nine years in the trade must qualify me for a competent witness upon the subject, but after an interval of more than thirty-three years, past scenes and transactions grow indistinct, and what I saw, and what I only heard related, may by this time have become so insensibly blended together that, in some cases, it may be difficult for me, if not impossible, to distinguish one from the other with absolute certainty. It is, however, my earnest desire that I put down nothing in writing which I would not, if requisite, confirm upon oath.

That part of the African shore, which lies between

the river Sierra Leone (lat. 8° 30' N) and Cape Palmas (lat. 4° 22' N) is usually known by the name of the Windward, or Grain, Coast, the extent (if my recollection does not fail me) being about three hundred miles. There was a fort upon Benee Island, in Sierra Leone, which formerly belonged to the old African Company; they also had a fort on an island in the River Sherbro, but the former was in private hands, and of the latter, scarcely the foundations were visible, when I first went to Africa. There is no fort, or factory, upon this coast under the sanction of our government. But there were, and probably still are, private traders resident at Benee Island, at the Bananoes, and at the Plantanes. The former of these is about twelve, and the latter twenty leagues, from Sierra Leone, to the south-east. By these persons the trade is carried on, in boats and shallops, thirty or forty leagues to the northward, in several rivers lying within the shoals of Rio Grande, but the most northerly place of trade for shipping is Sierra Leone, and all business there is chiefly transacted with the white men; from Sherbro to Cape Palmas buying and selling is directly with the natives. Though I have been on the Gold Coast, and beyond it as far as Cape Lopez (lat. 0.7° S) in the latitude of one or two degrees south, I profess no knowledge of the African trade but as it was conducted on the Windward Coast.

I am not qualified, as a minister of the Gospel, to consider the African slave trade merely in a political light; that disquisition more properly belongs to persons in civil life. My character as a minister simply allows me, and perhaps requires me, to observe that the best human policy is that which is connected with a reverential regard to Almighty God. Every plan which aims at the welfare of a nation, in defiance of his authority and laws will prove to be essentially defective and, if persisted in, ruinous. 'The righteous Lord loveth righteousness' (Psalm 11:7), and has engaged to plead the cause, and vindicate the wrongs, of the oppressed.

The slave trade was always unjustifiable, but inattention and interest prevented the evil from being perceived. At presently, however, the case is otherwise, as the mischiefs and evils connected with it have been, of late years, represented with such undeniable evidence, and are now so generally known, that there can hardly be one objection made to the wishes of thousands, perhaps millions, for the suppression of this trade – except upon the ground of political and financial expedience. Though were I even sure that a principal branch of public revenue depended upon the African trade (which I think is far from being the case), I would still feel myself bound to say to government, to parliament, and to the nation: 'It is not lawful to put it into the treasury, because it is the price of blood' (Matthew 27:6).

If an intelligent farmer has a large heap of good corn, he would not put a small quantity that is damaged into the rest, for the sake of increasing the heap. He knows that such an addition would spoil the whole. Therefore, God forbid that any supposed profit or advantage which we can derive from the groans, agonies, and blood of the poor Africans should draw down upon us his heavy curse upon all that we might otherwise honourably and comfortably possess.

The method I will use to consider the African trade will fall under two headings:

1. With regard to the effects, and losses, suffered among our own people.
2. As it concerns the blacks, or, as they are more contemptuously styled, the negro slaves.

Yet these two topics are so interwoven together that it will not be easy to keep them exactly separate.

1. As it concerns our own seamen and subjects.

The first point I shall mention is purely of political importance. How important should the lives of our fellow-subjects, our sailors be considered? And should the rapid loss of seamen deserve the attention of a maritime people? For the losses in the African trade are truly alarming. I admit that many die making their first voyage and, consequently, before they can perhaps be properly ranked as seamen. But then the neighbour-hoods of our seaports are continually drained of men and boys to replace those who die thus and, even if not accredited seamen, those that have died are still our brethren and countrymen, and subjects of the British government. Those on shipboard who survive, not accustomed to the climate, are liable to attacks of inflammatory fever, which, however, is not fatal unless other unfavourable circumstances are present. If these dangers particular to the coast are escaped, I think the sailors concerned might be as healthy as those on most other voyages, provided they keep from sleeping in the dews, from being much exposed to the rain, from drink, and especially from women.

But, considering the general disposition of our sailors, and the nature of the slave trade, these provisos are of little significance. For to be engaged the trade on the Windward Coast, sailors *must be* much exposed to the weather, especially where a great part of the cargo, the slaves, are procured by boats often sent to the distance of ninety to one hundred and twenty miles – often being away a month before they return. Also, many vessels arrive upon the coast before the rainy season (May to October), and if trade be scarce, the ships which arrive in this, the dry season, often remain till the rains return before they can complete their purchases. The rains, when they begin, are incessant night and day for weeks and months, while a proper shelter from them in an open boat is impracticable. I have myself in such a boat been five or six days together without a dry thread about me, sleeping or waking. Even during the fair season, tornadoes, violent storms of wind, thunder, and heavy rain are frequent, though seldom persisting. In fact, the boats seldom return without some of the crew ill of dangerous fevers or fluxes, occasioned either by the weather, or by unwholesome diet, such as the fruits and palm wine with which they are plentifully supplied by the natives.

English spirits, such as brandy and rum, the sailors cannot often procure in quantities as to hurt them, but given the chance they will procure these strong liquors and, as a single slave can hardly be purchased without such liquor, it is always at hand in the boats. And if what is taken from the casks or bottles that are for sale is replaced by water, they seem as full as they were before. While the blacks who buy these liquors are the losers by this adulteration, it is often the people who cheat them that are the greatest sufferers.

Women, likewise, contribute largely to the loss of our seamen. When the sailors are on shore, they often, from their known, thoughtless imprudence, involve themselves in quarrels with the natives over women, and are often killed upon the spot; otherwise they are frequently poisoned. On shipboard, they may be restrained from approaching the women slaves, and in some ships they are, but such restraint is far from being general, and depends much upon the disposition of the captain. When I was in the trade, I knew several commanders of African ships who were prudent, respectable men, and who maintained a proper discipline and regularity in their vessels as regards women slaves, but there were too many of a different character. In some ships, perhaps in the most, the licence allowed in this particular way was almost unlimited. Moral turpitude was seldom considered, and they who worked hard to do the ship's business might in other respects do what they pleased. These excesses, if they do not induce fevers, at least render the constitution unable to support them, and so lewdness, too, frequently terminates in death.

A further loss of our seamen is occasioned by slave insurrections. These, I believe, are always premeditated, for the men slaves are not reconciled to their confinement and treatment. These risings, if attempted, are seldom suppressed without considerable loss, and when they succeed, as they sometimes do, they can lead to the destruction of a whole ship's company. Seldom a year passes but we hear of one or more such catastrophes, and we likewise hear, sometimes, of whites and blacks together, in one common ruin, by the gunpowder taking fire and blowing up the ship and all aboard.

Taking all the above causes together, one fact is sure: that a great number of our seamen perish in the slave trade. I agree few ships, comparatively, are blown up, or totally seized by slaves, but some are. Of the rest, I have known some that have lost half their people, and some a larger proportion, from fevers and fluxes. I am far from saying that it is always, or even often, thus, but I believe that the lowest estimate of loss to be one fifth of any crew that goes from England to the coast of Africa, in ships which trade for slaves. I dare not depend too much upon my memory, as to the number of ships and men employed in the slave trade more than thirty years ago when I held my command, nor do I know what has been the state of the trade since. Therefore I shall not attempt to make calculations. But, as I cannot but help form some opinion upon the subject, I judge it probable that the collective sum of our seamen who go from all our ports to Africa yearly – taking Guinea in the extensive sense, from Gambia (13° 28' N) and stretching down to the coast of Angola (8° 50' S) – cannot be less than eight thousand. If upon an average a fifth part of these die, the annual loss to the country is fifteen hundred sailors, though I believe those who have made exact enquiries will deem my supposition to be very moderate. Thus much concerning the first evil, the loss of seamen and British subjects which the nation sustains through the African slave trade.

2. *The dreadful effects of the trade upon all, black and white, who are involved.*

The second point of importance to be considered in a political light is the effects of the trade on the minds of those that engage in it. There are doubtless exceptions, and I would willingly except myself. But in general I know of no method of getting money, not even that of highway robbery, which has a greater tendency to efface all moral sense, to rob the heart of every gentle and humane disposition, and to harden it, like steel, against all finer sensibilities.

Usually, about two-thirds of a cargo of slaves are males. Here you have one hundred and fifty or two hundred stout men, torn from their native land, many of whom never saw the sea before, much less a ship, and who often believe they are bought to be eaten. As well, they have probably the same natural prejudice against a white man, as we have against a black. Accordingly, we receive them on board from the first as our enemies, and as it is always taken for granted that they will attempt to gain their liberty, before their number exceeds, perhaps, ten or fifteen, they are all put in irons; in most ships, two and two together, and frequently ironed in such a way as prevents them standing or moving with ease. That is, instead of the right hand and a foot of one, to the left of the other, rather the hand and foot of each on the same side are fettered together, so that they neither move hand or foot, except but with great caution, and with perfect consent from both. Thus they must sit, walk and lie, for many months (sometimes for nine or ten) without any mitigation or relief, unless they are sick. As for exercise, in the daytime (if the weather be fine) they are upon deck, and as they are brought up by pairs, a chain is put through a ring upon their irons, and this is likewise locked down to the ringbolts, which are fastened at certain intervals upon the deck. At night they are always confined below.

These, and other precautions, are no more than necessary, especially as while the number of slaves increases, that of the people who are to guard them is simultaneously diminished by sickness, or death, or by being absent in the boats buying more slaves. So that sometimes not ten men can be mustered to watch, night and day, over two hundred, besides having all the other business of the ship to attend. Therefore, one unguarded hour, or minute, is sufficient to give the slaves the opportunity they are always waiting for. An attempt to rise upon the ship's company brings on instantaneous and horrid wars for, when they are once in motion, they are desperate, and where they do not conquer, they are seldom quelled without much bloodshed on both sides.

Sometimes, however, when the slaves are ripe for an insurrection, one of them will reveal the affair, and then it can be seen how necessity, in these small, but most absolute governments on board ship, enforces maxims directly contrary to the usual nature of things. For in this case, he who is a traitor is caressed, rewarded, and deemed an honest fellow, while the patriots who devised the plan, must be treated as villains, and then punished to intimidate the rest: punishments, which in their nature and degree, depend upon the sovereign will of the captain, some being content with inflicting such moderate punishment as may suffice for an example. But other captains relishing their unlimited power, instigated by revenge, and whose hearts by a long familiarity with the sufferings of slaves have become callous and insensible inflict terrible reprisals. I have seen slaves sentenced to unmerciful whippings, continued till the poor creatures have not had power left to groan and when hardly a sign of life has remained. I have seen them agonising for hours, I believe for days together, under the torture of the thumbscrews: a dreadful engine which, if the screw be turned by an unrelenting hand, can give intolerable anguish. There have also been instances in which cruelty has proceeded further, but these, I hope, are few, while I can only mention but one from my own knowledge. I have often heard about a captain, long since dead, who would boast of his conduct in a voyage when his slaves attempted to rise upon him. After he had suppressed the insurrection, he sat in judgement upon the insurgents and not only, in cold blood, adjudged several of them, I know not how many, to die, but studied, with no small attention, how to make death as excruciating to them as possible. For my readers' sake, I will suppress a recital of particulars.

Then there was a mate of a ship, ashore in the long-boat seeking slaves, who purchased a young woman who carried a fine child, about a year old, in her arms. In the night, the child cried much and disturbed the mate's sleep. He rose in great anger, and swore to the mother that if the child did not cease, he himself would silence it. The child continued to cry. At length he rose up a second time, tore the child from the mother, and threw it into the sea. The child was indeed soon silenced, but it was not so easy to pacify the woman (who was too valuable to be thrown overboard) and the mate was obliged to hear the sound of her constant lamentations till he could put her on board the main vessel.

I am persuaded that every tender mother who feasts her eyes and her mind on the infant in her arms will commiserate with this poor African. But why do I speak of one child, when we have all read the notoriously true, but melancholy story, of more than a hundred grown slaves being thrown into the sea because fresh water was scarce. This was to fix the loss of the slaves upon the insurers which otherwise, had the slaves died on board, must have fallen upon the owners of the vessel.

These instances are specimens of the spirit produced in its followers by the African trade, produced in men who were once no more destitute of the milk of human kindness than ourselves, and points to how much those long conversant with such scenes are liable to imbibe a spirit of ferociousness and savage insensibility, of which human nature, even as depraved as it usually is, is not ordinarily capable.

Hitherto, I have considered the condition of the men slaves only. From the women, there is no danger of insurrection, and they are carefully kept from the men, I mean, from the black men. But, in what I now have to offer concerning the slave women, I am far from including every ship. I speak not of what is absolutely universal, but of what is too commonly and, I am afraid, too generally prevalent.

I have already observed that the captain of an African ship, while upon the coast, is absolute in his command, and if he be humane, vigilant and determined, he has it in his power to protect the miserable, for scarcely any thing can be done on board the ship, without his permission, or connivance. But this power is too seldom exerted in favour of the poor women slaves and what is exacted upon, and from, them. When we hear of a town taken by storm, and given up to the ravages of an enraged and licentious army of wild and unprincipled Cossacks, perhaps no part of the distress affects a feeling mind more than the treatment to which the women are exposed. But the enormities frequently committed on an African ship, though equally flagrant, are little known here in England and are considered, there, in Africa, as only a matter of course.

When the women and girls are taken on board a ship, naked, trembling, terrified, perhaps almost exhausted with cold, fatigue and hunger, they are often exposed to the wanton rudeness of the white savages. The poor creatures may not understand the language they hear, but the looks and manner of the speakers are sufficiently intelligible. In imagination, the prey is divided upon the spot, and only reserved till opportunity offers. Where resistance or refusal would be utterly in vain, even the solicitation of consent is seldom thought of. But I forbear: this is not a subject for declamation. Facts like these, so certain, and so numerous, speak for themselves. Surely, if the advocates for the slave trade attempt to plead for it before the wives and daughters of our happy land, or before those who have wives or daughters of their own, they must lose their cause. I myself have seen in Sherbro, where I was most acquainted, many instances of feminine modesty, and even delicacy, which would not disgrace an English woman. Yet, such is the treatment which I have known permitted, if not encouraged, in many of our ships: these poor females abandoned, without restraint, to the lawless will of the first comer.

Even so, perhaps some hard-hearted pleader may suggest that such treatment would indeed be cruel in Europe, but that African women are negro savages who have no idea of the nicer sensations which obtain among civilised people. I contradict them in the strongest terms. I have lived long, and conversed much, among these supposed savages. I have often slept in their towns, in a house filled with goods for trade, with no person in the house but myself, and with no other door than a mat for security. Here, of course, in the same circumstances in this civilised nation, especially in London, no man in his senses would go without the precaution of sturdy doors, strongly locked and bolted.

Accustomed thus to despise, insult, and injure the slaves on board, it may be expected that the conduct of many of our people towards the natives with whom they trade is, as far as circumstances admit, equally familiar. And so it is. The Africans are considered as a people to be robbed with impunity. Every art is employed to deceive and wrong them, and he who is the biggest rogue is best regarded and understood to have the most of which to boast, for not an article that is capable of being tampered with by diminution or adulteration is delivered entire. The spirits, rum and brandy, have water added as a matter of course. False heads are put into the kegs that contain gunpowder so that, though the keg appears large, there is no more powder in it than in a much smaller keg. The rolls of linen and cotton cloths are opened, and two or three yards, according to the length of the piece, cut off, not from the end, but out of the middle where it is not so readily noticed, while sometimes a quarrel is fomented deliberately, which furnishes a pretext for detaining and carrying away one or more of the native traders as slaves.

The natives, then, are cheated in number, weight, measure, or quality, of whatever they purchase, in every possible way, and by habit and emulation, and an understandable marvellous dexterity, the natives, in their turn, in proportion to their commerce with the

Europeans, and (I am sorry to add) particularly with
the English, become jealous, insidious and revengeful.
They know with whom they deal, and come accordingly
prepared – although it must be said there are some ships
and boats which have treated them with punctuality,
and which they therefore trust. When they are misused
they will retaliate, if practicable, upon the next boat
that comes to the place from the same port, for their
vindictive temper is restrained by their ideas of justice,
so they will not often revenge an injury received from a
Liverpool ship upon one belonging to Bristol or London,
but rather wait with patience the arrival of one which
they suppose, by her sailing from the same English port,
has some connection with that which used them ill.
They are so quick at distinguishing our little local
differences of language and customs that before they
have been in any ship five minutes, and often before
they come on board, they know with certainty whether
it be from Bristol, Liverpool, or London.

Retaliation on their part, of course, demands reprisal
on ours. Thus, in one place or another, trade is often
suspended, all intercourse cut off, and things are in a
state of war till either necessity on the ship's part, or on
theirs, produces overtures of peace, and dictates the
price which the offending party must pay for it. But it
is a warlike peace. We trade under arms, and they are
furnished with long knives for, with a few exceptions,
the English and the Africans consider each other

consummate villains, with each always awaiting the opportunity to do mischief. In short, we have, I fear too deservedly, a very unfavourable character upon the coast. When I have charged a black with unfairness and dishonesty, he has often answered with an air of disdain, 'What! Do you think I am a white man?'

Such, then, is the nature of the slave trade, and such the school in which many thousands of our seamen are brought up. Can we then wonder at that impatience of subordination, and that disposition to mutiny, amongst them, which has been of late so loudly complained of, and so severely felt? Can not sound policy suggest some expedient here? Or can sound policy suggest any effectual expedient but the total suppression of a trade, which, like a poisonous root, diffuses its malignity into every branch?

Having dealt with the effect the trade has on our seamen and subjects, I will now consider its effects upon the blacks, especially those who come under our power as slaves. This may be considered under three heads:

1. How the slaves are acquired.
2. To what mortality are they subject.
3. The manner of disposing of the survivors.

1. How the slaves are acquired.

I will confine my remarks on this first head, the acquiring of the slaves, to the Windward Coast only, speaking most confidently of the trade at Sherbro, where I lived. But I must state that I think no other part of the Windward Coast equal to Sherbro in point of regularity and government. Here they have no men of great power or property as I am told there are upon the Gold Coast, and at Whidah and Benin. The Sherbro people live much in the patriarchal way. An old man usually presides in each town, whose authority depends more on his years than on his possessions, and he who is called king is not easily distinguished, either by state or wealth, from the rest. But the different districts, which seem in many respects independent of each other, are actually incorporated, and united, by means of an institution called the Purrow, the persons of which order, who are very numerous, seeming to much resemble the Druids who once presided in our island.

The Purrow has both the legislative and executive authority and, under their sanction, there is a police exercised, which is by no means contemptible. Private property is tolerably well secured, and violence is much suppressed. While everything that belongs to the Purrow is mysterious and severe, on the whole the Purrow has very good effects and any man, bonded or free, who will submit to be initiated into their mysteries, may be admitted to the order. It is therefore a kind of commonwealth and, indeed, perhaps few people enjoy a more simple political freedom than the inhabitants of Sherbro belonging to the Purrow, who are not slaves further than they are bound by their own institutions.

The state of slavery, among what we esteem as these wild barbarous people, is very much milder than in our own colonies. For as, on the one hand, they have no land in high cultivation, like our West India plantations, and therefore no call for that excessive, uninterrupted labour which exhausts our slaves so, on the other, no man is permitted to draw blood, even from a slave. If he does, he is liable to an inquisition, for the Purrow laws will not allow a private individual to shed blood. A man may sell his slave, if he pleases, but he may not wantonly abuse him. The laws likewise punish some species of theft with slavery, and in cases of adultery, which are very common, as polygamy is the custom of the country, both the woman and the man are liable to be sold for slaves.

Among these unenlightened blacks it is a general maxim that if a man steals, or breaks a moveable object, such as a musket for instance, the offence may be compensated by putting another musket in its place. But offences which cannot be repaid in kind, such as adultery, admit of no satisfaction till the injured person declares he is satisfied. So if a rich man seduces the wife of a poor man, the poor man has it in his power to send for every article in the rich man's house, one by one, until the poor man declares, 'I have enough.' The only alternative for the rich man is personal slavery.

So while I suppose bribery and influence must be taken into account in Guinea, as in some other countries, their laws, in the main, seem wise and good. Therefore, I believe, many of the slaves purchased in Sherbro, and probably upon the whole Windward Coast, are convicted convicts, but I also understand that the arrival of our ships and their desire for our goods are motives which influence their laws to an extreme which would not be exacted if they were left to themselves.

But slaves are the staple article of the traffic, and though a considerable number may have been born near the sea, I believe the bulk of them are acquired from afar. I have reason to think that some travel more than a thousand miles before they reach the sea coast. Whether there may be convicts among these likewise, or what proportion they may bear to those who are taken as prisoners of war, it is impossible to know, but I judge the principal source of slaves to be the wars which prevail among the natives. Sometimes, if these wars break out between those who live near the sea, the English and other Europeans are charged with fomenting them, I believe (so far as concerns the Windward Coast) unjustly. That they would do it, if they could, I doubt not, but I do not think they can have opportunity, nor is it needful they should interfere. Do not thousands in our own country constantly wish for war because they fatten upon its spoils?

Human nature is much the same in every place and few people will be willing to allow that the negroes in Africa are better than themselves. Supposing, therefore, they wish for European goods, may not they wish to purchase them from a ship just arrived? Of course, they must wish for slaves to go to market with, and if they have not slaves, and think themselves strong enough to invade their neighbours, they will probably wish for war. Once wished for, how easy to find, or make, pretexts for breaking an inconvenient peace, or (after the example of greater heroes of Christian name) to simply invade without condescending to assign any reasons. I verily believe that the far greater part of the wars in Africa would cease, if the Europeans would cease to tempt them by offering goods for slaves, and though they do not bring legions into the field, their wars are very bloody, and I believe the captives reserved for sale as slaves are fewer than the slain.

I have not sufficient data to warrant calculation, but I suppose not less than one hundred thousand slaves are exported annually from all parts of Africa, and that more than one half of these are exported in English ships. If but an equal number are killed in war, and if many of these wars are kindled by the incentive of capturing slaves for the trade, what an annual accumulation of blood must there be, crying against the nations of Europe and particularly against our own! I have often been gravely told that the Africans, however hardly treated, deserve little compassion because they are a people so destitute of natural affection it is common among them for parents to sell the children, and the children the parents, a charge of this kind, I think, being offered against them by the respectable author of *Spectacle of Nature*. But he must have been misinformed. I never heard of one instance of either, while I used the coast.

One article more, upon this first head regarding slave acquisition is the kidnapping, or stealing, of free people. Some people suppose that the ship trade is rather the stealing than the buying of slaves. But there is enough to lay to the charge of the ships without accusing them falsely. The slaves, in general, are bought and paid for. Sometimes, when goods are lent or trusted on shore, the trader voluntarily leaves a free person, perhaps his own son, as hostage or pawn for the payment and, in case of default, the hostage is carried off and sold which, however hard upon him, being the consequence of a free stipulation cannot be deemed unfair. There have been instance of unprincipled captains who, at the close of what they supposed their last voyage, and when they had no intention of revisiting the coast, have detained and carried away free people with them, and left the next ship that should come from the same port to risk the consequences. But these actions, I hope, and believe, are not common.

With regard to the natives, to steal a free man or woman and to sell them on board a ship would, I think, be a more difficult and more dangerous attempt in Sherbro than in London. But I have no doubt that the traders who come from the interior parts of Africa at a great distance find opportunity in the course of their journey to pick up stragglers whom they may meet in their way. This branch of oppression and robbery would likewise fail if the temptation to it were removed.

2. *Slave mortality in the middle passage.*

I have, to the best of my knowledge, pointed out the principal sources of that immense supply of slaves which furnishes so large an exportation from the shores of Africa every year, and have no doubt that, if all that were taken on board the ships were to survive the voyage, and be landed in good health, possibly the English, French, and Dutch islands and colonies would be soon overstocked, and fewer ships would sail to the coast. But a large abatement must be made for mortality. After what I have already said of their treatment I shall, now that I am again to consider them on board the ships, confine myself to this point.

In the Portuguese ships which trade from Brazil to the Gold Coast and Angola, I believe, a heavy mortality is not frequent. The slaves have room, they are not put in irons (I speak from information only) and are humanely treated. With our ships, however, the one great object is to be full! When a ship is there, it is thought desirable she should take as many as possible. The trade cargo carried to the coast in an English vessel of a hundred tons, or a little more, is calculated to purchase from two hundred and twenty to two hundred and fifty slaves.

The lodging rooms below the deck are three – one for the men, one for boys, one for women, together with a place for the sick. These rooms are sometimes more than five feet high, and sometimes less, and even this height is divided towards the middle, for the slaves lie in two rows, one above the other, on each side of the ship, close to each other like books upon a shelf. I have known them so close that the shelf would not, easily, contain one more. I have known a white man sent down, among the men, to lay them in these rows to the greatest advantage, so that as little space as possible might be lost. Let it also be observed that these poor creatures, cruelly cramped for want of room, are likewise in irons, for the most part both hands and feet, and two together, which makes it difficult for them to turn or move, to attempt either to rise or to lie down, without hurting themselves, or each other. Nor is the motion of the ship, especially her heeling, or stooping to one side when under sail, to be omitted. For this, as they lie athwart, or across the ship, adds to the great uncomfortableness of their lodging, especially to those who lie on the leeward, or leaning, side of the vessel: 'Dire is the tossing, deep the groans.'

The heat and the smell of these rooms when the weather will not admit of the slaves being brought upon deck, and of having their rooms cleaned every day, would be almost insupportable to a person not accustomed to them. If kept down by the weather to breathe a hot and corrupted air, sometimes for a week, this, added to the galling of their irons, and the despondency which seizes their spirits, soon becomes fatal, and every morning, perhaps, more instances than one are found of the living and the dead, like the captives of Mezentius, fastened together.

Epidemical fevers and fluxes, which fill the ship with noisome and noxious effluvia, also often break out, infecting seamen and slaves, the oppressors and the oppressed falling by the same stroke. I believe nearly one half of the slaves on board have sometimes died, and that the loss of a third part, in these circumstances is not unusual. The ship in which I was mate left the coast with two hundred and eighteen slaves on board, and though we were not much affected by epidemical disorders, I find, by my journal of that voyage (now before me) that we buried sixty-two on our passage to South Carolina, exclusive of those who died before we left the coast, of which I have no account.

I believe, upon an average, between the more healthy and the more sickly voyages, and including all contingencies, a fourth of the whole purchase may be allotted to the article of mortality. That is, if the English ships purchase sixty thousand slaves annually, upon the whole extent of the coast, the annual loss of lives cannot be much less than fifteen thousand. Of course, if the slaves and their rooms can be constantly aired, and they are not detained too long on board, perhaps there are not many die, but the contrary is often their lot.

3. Manner of disposing of the survivors.

I am now to speak of the survivors. When ships make the land (usually the West India Islands) and have their port in view after having been four, five, six weeks, or longer at sea (which depends much upon the time that passes before they can get into the permanent trade winds which blow from the north-east and east across the Atlantic), then, and not before, they venture to release the men slaves from their irons. These, at the sight of land, and their freedom from long and painful confinement, are generally usually excited to a degree of alacrity, and a transient feeling of joy: 'The prisoner leaps to lose his chains.' But this joy is short-lived, indeed.

The condition of the unhappy slaves is a continual progress from bad to worse. Their case is truly pitiable from the moment they are in a state of slavery in their own country. Yet this previous state of slavery might be deemed a state of ease and liberty, compared to the situation they have endured on board the ship, and yet again, perhaps they would wish to spend the remainder of their days on shipboard, could they know the nature of the servitude which awaits them on shore – and that the dreadful hardships and sufferings they have already endured, will, for most of them only terminate in excessive toil, hunger, and the excruciating tortures of the cart whip, inflicted at the caprice of an unfeeling overseer, proud of the power allowed him of punishing whom, and when, and how, he pleases.

I hope the slaves in our islands are better treated now than they were at the time when I was in the trade. Even then, I know, there were slaves who, under the care and protection of humane masters, were comparatively happy. But I saw and heard enough to satisfy me that conditions, in general, for all slaves were wretched to the extreme. However, my stays in Antigua and St Christopher's (the only islands I visited) were too short to qualify me for saying much from my own certain knowledge upon this painful subject. Nor is it needful: enough has been offered by several respectable writers, who have had opportunity of collecting surer, and fuller, information.

One thing I cannot omit, which was told me by the gentleman to whom my ship was consigned, at Antigua in the year 1751, and who was himself a planter. He said that calculations had been made with all possible exactness to determine which was the preferable (that is, the more economical) method of managing slaves: whether to give them moderate work, plenty of provisions, and such treatment as might enable them to protract their lives to old age, or by rigorously straining their strength to the utmost, with little relaxation, bad fare, and hard usage, to wear them out before they became useless and unable to do service, and then to buy new ones to fill up their places. He further said that the calculations favoured the latter mode as being much the cheaper, and that he himself knew of several estates on Antigua where it was seldom that any slave had lived above nine years.

When the slaves are landed for sale (for those coming to the Leeward Islands are usually sold on shore), it may happen that after a long separation in different parts of the ship, when they are brought together in one place some who are related may recognise each other. If upon such a meeting pleasure should be felt, it can be but momentary. The sale disperses them wide, to different parts of the island, or to different islands. Husbands and wives, parents and children, brothers and sisters, must suddenly part again, probably to meet no more.

Finally, after a careful perusal of what I have written, weighing every paragraph distinctly, I find nothing to retract. As it is not easy to write altogether with coolness upon this business, and especially not easy for me, who have formerly been so deeply engaged in it, I have been jealous, lest the warmth of my imagination might have insensibly seduced me to aggravate and overcharge some of the horrid features which I have attempted to delineate of the African trade. But, upon a strict review, I am satisfied I have apprised the reader that I write from memory after an interval of more than thirty years. But at the same time, I believe, many things which I saw, heard and felt upon the coast of Africa are so deeply engraven in me that I could hardly be capable of forgetting them, or greatly mistaking them, while I am capable of remembering anything. I am certainly not guilty of wilful misrepresentation. And, upon the whole, I affirm before the Great Searcher of hearts, in whose presence I write, and before whom I, and my readers, must all shortly appear, that (with the restrictions and exceptions I have made) I have advanced nothing but what, to the best of my judgement and conscience, is the truth. I have likewise written without solicitation, simply from the motive I have already assigned: a conviction that the share I have formerly had in the trade binds me, in conscience, to throw what light I am able upon the subject now it is likely to become a point of parliamentary investigation.

No one can have less interest in it than I have at present, further than I am interested by feelings of humanity, and by a regard for the honour, and welfare, of my country. Though unwilling to give offence to a single person, in such a cause I own not to be afraid of offending many by declaring the truth if, indeed, there can be many whom even interest can prevail upon to contradict the common sense of mankind, by still pleading for a commerce so iniquitous, cruel, oppressive and destructive as the African slave trade!

Part II

An Authentic Narrative of Some Remarkable and
Interesting Particulars in the Life of John Newton

1. Childhood and youth.

Letter I

To the Reverend Mr Haweis.

Dear Sir,

I have no doubt you have, at times, reflected on that promise made to the Israelites: 'You shall remember the way which the Lord your God has led you in the wilderness these forty years, that he might humble you, testing you, to know what was in your heart, whether you would keep his commandments or not.' But they, who were in the wilderness, surrounded with difficulties, frequently lost sight of God's gracious purposes, and were much discouraged by their long and difficult journey.

To compose and animate their minds, Moses suggested to them that there was a future happy time drawing near when their journey and warfare should be finished and that they should soon be put in possession of the promised land, when it would give them pleasure to look back upon what they now found so uneasy to bear: 'Thou shalt remember all the way by which the

Lord led thee through this wilderness.' The importance and comfort of these words is still greater if we consider them in a spiritual sense as being addressed to all who are passing through the wilderness of this world; and who, by faith in God, are seeking an eternal faith which cannot be shaken. And when a time comes when our warfare shall be over, and our light increased; then with what transports of love shall we look back upon the way by which the Lord led us!

We shall then see and acknowledge that mercy and goodness directed every step; that what in our ignorance we once called adversities and evils, were in reality blessings, which we could not have done well without; that nothing befell us without a cause; and that no trouble continued longer than our case required. In a word, that our many afflictions were each among the means employed by divine grace to bring us to the possession of that glory which the Lord has prepared for his people. If we look upon the years of our past life, and compare the dispensations we have been brought through, how wonderfully one thing has been connected with another, we may see that what we now number amongst our greatest advantages, perhaps took their first rise from incidents which we thought hardly worth our notice, and consider these things indisputable proof, from the narrow circle of our own concerns, of the Providence of God that watches over his people from the earliest moment of their life, and guards them through their state of ignorance, till at length events and impressions bring them to the knowledge of him, and of themselves.

I am persuaded that every believer will, upon due reflection, see enough in his own case to confirm this remark, though not all in the same degree. The outward circumstances of many have known but little variety in life, and their inward change has been effected in a secret way, unnoticed by others, and almost unperceived by themselves; the Lord has spoke to them not in thunder and tempest, but with a still, small voice. In others he seems to suffer the natural rebellion and wickedness of their hearts to have full scope, and while sinners of less note are cut off with little warning, these others are spared, though, as it were, sinning with a high hand as if studying their own destruction. At length, when all that know them are expecting to hear that they are made signal instance of divine vengeance, the Lord (whose thoughts are high above ours) is pleased to pluck them as brands out of the fire and to make them monuments of his mercy and they are, beyond expectation, pardoned and changed – something which indicates a divine power and the Lord's doing; it is marvellous in the eyes of all those not blinded by prejudice and unbelief.

Such was the persecuting Saul: his heart was full of enmity against Jesus of Nazareth, and he therefore persecuted and made havoc of his disciples. He had been a terror to the church in Jerusalem, and was going to Damascus with the same views; he was yet breathing out threatenings and slaughter against all that loved the Lord Jesus. He thought little of the mischief he had hitherto done; he was engaged for the suppression of the whole sect and hurrying from house to house, from place to place, he carried menaces in his look, and repeated threatenings with every breath. Such was his spirit and temper, when the Lord Jesus, whom he hated and opposed, checked him in the height of his rage, called this bitter persecutor to the honour of an apostle, and inspired him with great zeal and earnestness to preach that faith which he had so lately destroyed.

Nor are we without remarkable displays of the same sovereign efficacious grace in our own times – I may particularly mention the instance of the late Colonel Gardiner. If any real satisfaction could be found in a single course, he would have met with it; for he pursued the experiment with all possible advantages – he was habituated to evil, and many uncommon, almost miraculous deliverances, made no impression upon him. Yet he, too, was made willing by God's grace, and the bright example of his later life, illustrated and diffused by the account published since his death, has afforded an occasion of much praise to God, and much comfort to his people.

After the mention of such names, can you permit me, sir, to add my *own*? If I do, it must be with a very humbling distinction. That whereas these once eminent sinners proved eminent Christians, with me, alas, the parallel greatly fails in that I have made very unsuitable returns for what I have received. But if the question is only concerning the patience and long-suffering of God in favour of pardoning the most enormous and aggravated transgressions of an unworthy sinner; in these respects I know no case more extraordinary than my own, and indeed, most persons to whom I have related my story, have thought it worthy of being preferred.

I never gave any succinct account in writing of the Lord's dealings with me till very lately, for I was deterred, on the one hand, by the great difficulty of writing properly when *self* is concerned; on the other, by the ill use which persons of corrupt and perverse minds are often known to make of such instances, our Lord cautioning us not to 'cast pearls before swine'. The pearls of a Christian are, perhaps, his choice experiences of the Lord's power and love, not at all adventures to be made public lest we give occasion to earthly and grovelling souls to profane what they cannot understand.

These were the chief reasons of my backwardness, but a few weeks since I obliged a much respected friend and sent him a relation of my life at large, in a series of eight letters. This event occasioned what I little expected; I wrote to one person, but my letters fell into many hands. Amongst others, I find they have reached your notice; and instead of finding me tedious and circumstantial (the fault I feared), you are pleased to desire still more distinct detail – and as you and others of my friends feel my compliance with this request may be attended with some good effects in promoting praise to our adorable Redeemer, or to confirm the faith of some or other of his people, I am willing to obey. If God may be glorified, and his children instructed, by what I have to declare, I shall be satisfied and content to leave all other possible consequences in his hands.

I will again have recourse to memory, as I retained no copies of the letters you saw. So far as I can recollect them, I will relate what I then wrote, but shall not affect a needless variety of manner because those have been already perused by many. I may perhaps in some places, when repeating the same facts, express myself in nearly the same words; yet, according to your desire, will endeavour to make this relation more explicit and particular than the former. I hope you will likewise excuse me, if I do not merely confine myself to narration, but sometimes interpose such reflections as may offer while I am writing. You have signified your intentions of communicating what I send you to others, and so I must not, on this account, affect a conciseness and correctness which is not my natural talent, lest the whole should appear dry and constrained. I shall therefore (if possible) think only of you, writing with a confidence and freedom which I feel your friendship and candour deserve. This first letter may stand as a preface, and I purpose, as far as I can, to cancel all other engagements until I have completed the task you have assigned me.

In the meantime, I entreat the assistance of your prayers, that in my poor attempts I have a single eye to his glory, who was pleased to call me out of the darkness into the light of his gospel.

I am, with sincere respect, dear Sir,

Your obliged and affectionate servant.

12 January 1763

Letter II

Reverend Sir,

I can sometimes feel a pleasure in repeating the grateful acknowledgment of David, 'O Lord, I am thy servant, the son of thine handmaid', for my mother was a pious Christian Dissenter in communion with the late Dr Jennings. I was her only child, and as she was of weak constitution, and a retiring manner, almost her whole employment was the care of my education. At a time when I could not be more than three years of age she taught me English with so much success (I had something of a forward turn) that when I was four years old, I could read in any common book that was offered. She also stored my memory, which was then very retentive, with many valuable pieces – portions of scripture, catechisms, hymns, and poems – so that I had little inclination to the noisy sports of children, but was best pleased when in her company, and was as willing to learn as she was to teach.

How far that best education fell short of reaching my heart will appear in the sequel of my history; yet I think, for the encouragement of pious parents to form their children's minds, I may properly propose myself as an instance. Though in process of time I sinned away all these early advantages, yet they were for a great while a restraint upon me; they returned again and again, and it was very long before I could wholly shake them off, and when the Lord at length did open my eyes, I found a great benefit in the recollection of them. My mother observed my early progress with peculiar pleasure, and intended from the first to bring me up with a view to the ministry, if the Lord should so incline my heart. In my sixth year I began to learn Latin, but before long the intended plan of my education was broken short. The Lord's designs were far beyond the views of an earthly parent and he therefore overruled her purpose by depriving me of this excellent parent when I was something under seven years old. I was born 24 July 1725, and she died on the eleventh day of that month, 1732.

My father was then at sea, being a commander in the Mediterranean trade at that time. He came home the following year, soon after married again, and thus I passed into different hands. I was well treated in all other respects, but the loss of my mother's instructions was never repaired. I was now permitted to mingle with careless and profane children, and soon began to learn their ways. Soon after, I was sent to a boarding school in Essex, where the severity of the master almost broke my spirit and relish for books, forgetting the first principles and rules of arithmetic which my mother had taught me. I stayed there two years: in the last of the two, a new usher coming who suited my temper, I took to Latin with great eagerness, so that before I was ten years old, I gained first post in the second class which, in that school, read Tully and Virgil. I believe I was pushed forward too fast, and not being properly grounded I soon lost all I had learned (for I left school in my tenth year to go to sea with my father.) And when, long afterwards, I undertook the Latin language from books, I had little advantage from what I had learned before.

My father was a man of remarkable good sense, and having a knowledge of the world took great care of my morals, but could not supply my mother's part. Having been educated in Spain, he always observed an air of distance and severity to me, which overawed and discouraged my spirit, and I was always in fear when before him, giving him the less influence over me. From 1736 to the year 1742 I made several voyages, but with considerable intervals between, which were chiefly spent in the country, excepting a few months in my fifteenth year, when I was put into a very advantageous position at Alicante in Spain, but my unsettled behaviour and impatience rendered that design abortive, as at that period my temper and conduct were exceedingly various, and easily received very ill impressions.

But I was often disturbed with convictions, and when, among other books, Bennet's *Christian Oratory* often came my way, although I understood but little of it, the course of life therein recommended appeared very desirable, and I began to pray and read scripture, and keep a sort of diary until I was presently religious in my own eyes – though this seeming goodness had no solid foundation, but passed away like a morning cloud, or the early dew. Growing weary, I gradually gave it up, and instead of prayer learned to curse and blaspheme, and behave exceedingly wicked when not under my parents' view – and all before I was twelve years old. About that time I had a dangerous fall from a horse, being thrown within a few inches of a newly cut hedgerow. I got no hurt, but could not avoid noticing a gracious Providence in my deliverance, for had I fell upon the hedge stakes, I had inevitably been killed. My conscience suggesting to me the dreadful consequences of appearing before God in such a state, I broke off from profane practices and appeared quite altered, but it was not long before I declined again.

These struggles between sin and conscience were often repeated, but every relapse sunk me still into greater depths of wickedness. I was once roused by the loss of an intimate companion. We had agreed to go on board a man-of-war (I think it was on a Sunday) but I providentially came too late; the boat was overset, and he and several others were drowned. I was invited to the funeral and was exceedingly affected, to think that by a delay of a few minutes (which much angered me, till I saw the event) my life had been preserved. However, this likewise was soon forgot. In brief, though I cannot distinctly relate particulars, I think I took up and laid aside a religious profession three or four times before I was sixteen years of age, but all this while my heart was insincere. I often saw a necessity of religion as a means of escaping hell, but I loved sin, and was unwilling to forsake it and would always rush into folly with little remorse.

My last reform was the most remarkable, both for degree and continuance and in which I did everything that might be expected from a person entirely ignorant of God's righteousness, but desirous to establish his own. I spent the greatest part of every day in reading the Scriptures, meditation and prayer. I fasted often; I even abstained from animal food for three months; I would hardly answer a question, for fear of speaking an idle word. I bemoaned my former miscarriages very earnestly, sometimes with tears. In short, I became an ascetic, and endeavoured, so far as my situation would permit, to renounce society, that I might avoid temptation. I continued in this serious mood (I cannot give it a higher title) for more than two years, but it was a poor religion, and left me in many respects under the power of sin, in that it only made me gloomy, stupid, unsociable, and useless.

Such was my frame of my mind when I became acquainted with Lord Shaftesbury. I saw the second volume of his *Characteristics* in a petty shop at Middleburg in Holland. The title allured me, and the style and manner gave me great pleasure in reading, especially the second piece, which his Lordship with great propriety entitled a 'Rhapsody'. Nothing could have been more suited to the romantic turn of my mind than this pompous declamation, the design and tendency of which I was not aware. I thought the author a most religious person, and that I had only to follow him and be happy. Thus, with fine words and fair speeches my simple heart was beguiled and I read and reread the 'Rhapsody' till I could nearly repeat it verbatim from beginning to end. No immediate effect followed, but it operated like a slow poison, preparing the way for all that followed.

It was now December 1742. I was then lately returned from a voyage, and my father not intending me for the sea again, was thinking how to settle me in the world. He thought of commerce, but I had little spirit for business, being more fond of a visionary scheme of things – a contemplative life with a medley of religion, philosophy, and indolence – rather than industrious application. At length a merchant in Liverpool, Mr Manesty, an intimate of my father's (to whom, as the instrument of God's goodness, I have since been chiefly indebted for all my earthly comforts), proposed to send me to Jamaica, and to charge himself with the care of my future fortune. I consented to this, and was upon the point of setting out the following week for Liverpool, when my father sent me on some business to a place a few miles beyond Maidstone in Kent. This little journey, which was to have been only for three or four days, occasioned that sudden and remarkable turn of which you desire a more particular account. Indeed, 'the way of man is not in himself; it is not in man that walketh to direct his steps.'

I am affectionately,

Yours in the best bonds.

13 January 1763

2. I fall in love. The beginnings of my sea
career. Impressment. Desertion to see my love. I
am retaken and publicly flogged and disrated. I
exchange into a Guineaman.

Letter III

Dear Sir,

A few days before my journey into Kent I received an
invitation to visit a family in that county who were not
only distant relations, but very intimate friends of my
dear mother. She had, in fact, died in their house, but
there being a coolness occasioned by my father's second
marriage, I had heard nothing of them for many years.
But as my road lay within half a mile of their house, I
obtained my father's leave to call on them.

I was, initially, very indifferent about it, and thought
of passing them by. All intercourse between the families
had been long broken off; I was shortly going into a
foreign country, I could only stop to pay a hasty visit,
etc., and should not have thought of it myself but for
their invitation, not having been invited any time before.
Thus the circumstances were precarious – however, I
went. But once there, I was known at first sight before I
could tell my name, and met with the kindest reception,
as the child of a dear deceased friend, and the ensuing
events were in the highest degree extraordinary.

I fall in love

My friends had two daughters. The eldest (as I understood some years afterwards) had, from the time of her birth, been often considered by her mother and mine as a future wife for me. I know, indeed, that intimate friends amuse themselves with such prospects for their children, but also that they miscarry much oftener than succeed. I do not say that my mother predicted what was to happen, yet there was something remarkable in the manner of its taking place. For at almost first sight of this girl (for she was then under fourteen), I was impressed with an affection for her which never abated or lost its influence on my heart for a single moment from that hour. In degree, it equalled all that writers of romances have ever imagined; in duration, it was unalterable. Even when I lost all sense of religion and reason, my regard for her was always the same, and none of the scenes of misery and wickedness I afterwards experienced ever banished her a single hour from my waking thoughts for the seven following years.

Give me leave, sir, to reflect a little upon this un-expected incident, and to consider its influence upon my future life, and how far it was subservient to the views of Divine Providence concerning me, which seem to have been twofold: that by being given up for a while to the consequences of my own wilfulness, and afterwards reclaimed by a high hand, my case, so far as it should be known, might be both a warning and an encouragement to others. In the first place, hardly anything less than this violent and commanding passion would have been sufficient to awaken me from the dull melancholy habit I had contracted. I was, alas, a misanthrope, notwithstanding I so much admired the pictures of virtue and benevolence as drawn by Lord Shaftesbury; but now my reluctance to active life was completely overturned, and I was willing to be, or do, anything which might guarantee the accomplishment of my wishes at some future time. Further, when I afterwards made a shipwreck of faith, hope, and conscience, my love of this person was the only remaining principle which in any degree supplied their place, and it was only the bare possibility of my seeing her again that restrained me from the most horrid designs against myself and others.

But there were also the ill effects that it brought upon me to counterbalance these advantages. That interval usually styled the time of courtship is indeed a pleasing part of life, where there is a mutual affection, the comfort of friends, a reasonable prospect as to settlement, and the whole conducted in a prudential manner, and in subordination to the will and fear of God. When these things are present, it is a blessing to be susceptive to the tender passions, but when they are wanting, what we call *love* is the most tormenting passion in itself, and the most destructive in its consequences that can be named, and they *were* wanting in my case. I durst not mention my feelings to her friends, or to my own, nor indeed for a considerable time – to *herself*. As I could make no firm proposals, it therefore remained as a dark fire, locked up in my own breast, which gave me a constant uneasiness. Also, introducing an idolatrous regard to a fellow creature greatly weakened my sense of religion, and made way for the entrance of many infidel principles, and though it seemed to promise great things as an incentive to diligence and activity in life, in reality it performed nothing. I often formed mighty projects in my mind of what I would do or suffer for her; yet while I could have her company, I was incapable of doing anything else. Still less did it regulate my manners as it did not seem to prevent me from engaging in a long train of excess and riot, utterly unworthy the honourable pretensions I had formed. Although, through the wonderful interposition of divine goodness, the maze of my follies was at length unravelled, and my wishes crowned in a manner that overpaid my sufferings, yet I would not go through the same series of trouble again to possess all the treasures of both the Indies. I have enlarged more than I intended on this point, as perhaps these papers may be useful to caution others against indulging an ungovernable passion. To sow the wind is indeed to reap the whirlwind.

My heart being now being riveted to a particular object, everything had to be considered in a new light. I concluded it would be absolutely impossible to live at such a distance from her as Jamaica, for a term of four or five years, and therefore determined I would not go. As I could not bear to acquaint my father with the true reason, or to invent a false one, I therefore stayed three weeks, instead of three days, till, as I thought (and as it proved) the ship had sailed. I then returned to London. I had highly displeased my father by this disobedience, but he was more easily reconciled than I expected, and in a little time I sailed with a friend of his to Venice.

On this voyage I was exposed to the company and ill example of the common sailors, among whom I ranked, and opportunity presenting every day, I once more began to relax from the sober order which I had observed for more than two years. Although I did not turn profligate, I began making large strides towards a total apostasy from God. The most remarkable check and alarm I received (and, for what I know, the last) was by a dream, which made a very strong, though not an abiding impression, upon my mind. But I do not doubt, from what I have seen since, that it had a direct and easy application to my own circumstances, to the dangers in which I was about to plunge myself, and to the unmerited deliverance and mercy which God would be pleased to afford me in the time of my distress.

The scene presented to my imagination was the harbour of Venice, where we had lately been. It was night, and my watch upon deck. As I was walking to and fro by myself, a person came to me (I do not remember from whence), and brought me a ring, with an express charge to keep it carefully, assuring me that while I preserved that ring I should be happy and successful, but if I lost or parted with it I must expect nothing but trouble and misery. I accepted the present and the terms willingly, highly satisfied to have my happiness in my own keeping. I had just put the ring on my finger when a second person came to me, and observing the ring, took occasion to ask me some questions concerning it. I readily told him its virtues, and his answer expressed a surprise at my expecting such effects from a ring, at length urging me in direct tones to throw it away. At first I was shocked at the proposal, but his insinuations prevailing, I began to reason and doubt myself, and at last plucked it off my finger, and dropped it over the ship's side into the water, which it had no sooner touched, than I saw, at the same instant, a terrible fire burst out of the Alps mountains which appeared at some distance behind the city of Venice.

I perceived too late my folly, and my tempter with an air of insult informed me that all the mercy God had reserved for me was in that ring which I had now wilfully thrown away. I understood that I must now go with him to the burning mountains, and that all the flames I saw were kindled for me. I trembled, and was in such great agony it was surprising I did not awake, but my dream continued, and when I thought myself upon the point of departure, already self-condemned, suddenly either a third person, or the same who brought the ring at first (I was not certain which), came to me and demanded the cause of my grief. I confessed that I had ruined myself wilfully, and deserved no pity. He blamed my rashness, and asked should I be wiser, supposing I had my ring again? I could hardly answer this, for I thought it was gone beyond recall. Indeed, I had not time to answer, before I saw this friend go down under the water, soon to return, bringing the ring with him, at which point the flames in the mountains were extinguished, and my seducer left me.

With joy and gratitude I approached my kind deliverer to receive the ring again, but he refused to return it, and spoke to this effect: 'If you should be entrusted with this ring again, you would soon bring yourself into the same distress; you are not able to keep it, but I will preserve it for you, and *whenever* it is needful, will produce it in your behalf.' Upon this I awoke, in a state of mind not to be described: I could hardly eat or sleep, or transact my necessary business for two or three days. But the impression soon wore off, and in a little time I totally forgot it; and I think it hardly occurred to my mind again, till several years afterwards.

It will appear, in the course of these papers, that a time came when I found myself in circumstances very nearly resembling those suggested by this extraordinary dream, when I stood helpless and hopeless upon the brink of an awful eternity, and I doubt not, but had the eyes of my mind been then opened, I should have seen my grand enemy who had seduced me wilfully to renounce and cast away my religious profession, and to involve myself in the most complicated crimes; I say, I should probably have seen him pleased with my agonies, and waiting for a permission to seize and bear away my soul to his place of torment. I should perhaps have seen likewise that Jesus, whom I had persecuted and defied, rebuking the adversary, challenging me for his own as a brand plucked out of the fire, and saying, 'Deliver him from going down into the pit; I have found a ransom.' However, though I saw not these things, I found the benefit; I obtained mercy. The Lord answered for me in the day of my distress and, blessed be his name, he who restored the ring (or what was signed by it) vouchsafes to keep it.

Nothing very remarkable occurred in the following part of that voyage. I returned home in December 1743, and soon after repeated my visit to Kent, where I protracted my stay in the same imprudent manner, which again disappointed my father's designs and almost provoked him to disown me.

Before any thing suitable offered again, I was impressed (owing entirely to my own thoughtless conduct, which was all of a piece), and put on board a tender. This was at a critical juncture, when the French fleets were hovering upon our coasts, and my father was unable to procure my release. In a few days I was sent on board the *Harwich*, man-of-war, at the Nore: I entered here upon quite a new scene of life, and endured much hardship for about a month. As war was daily expected, and my father willing that I should remain in the Navy, he procured me a recommendation to the captain, who took me upon the quarterdeck as a midshipman. I now had an easy life as to externals, and might have gained respect, but my mind was unsettled, and I now met with companions who completed the ruin of my principles, until my delight and habitual practice was wickedness.

My chief intimate was a person of good natural talents, and much observation: the greatest master of what is called the 'free-thinking scheme' I remember to have met with, and who knew how to insinuate his sentiments in the most plausible way – and his zeal being equal to his address, he could hardly have laboured more in the cause if he had expected to gain heaven by it. Yet this man, whom I honoured as my master, and whose practice I adopted so eagerly, perished in the same way as I expected to have done. His vessel being overtaken by a great storm in a voyage from Lisbon, a great sea broke on board and swept him into eternity, though the vessel and people escaped. Thus the Lord spares or punishes! But to return – I was fond of his company, and having myself a smattering of learning, was eager enough to show what I had read. Perceiving that I had not wholly broke through the restraints of conscience, he did not shock me at first with too broad intimations of his design; rather, he spoke favourably of religion. But when he had gained my confidence, he began to speak plainer, and so plied me with objections and arguments that my depraved heart was soon gained, and I entered into his plan with all my spirit. Thus, like an unwary sailor who puts to sea just before a rising storm, I renounced the hopes and comforts of the gospel, at the very time when every other comfort was about to fail me.

In December 1744 the *Harwich* was in the Downs, bound to the East Indies. The captain gave me liberty to go ashore for a day, but without consulting prudence or consequences, I took horse, and following the dictates of my reckless passion, I went to take a last leave of her I loved. You have in your letters to me desired a more explicit account of the state and progress of my courtship, as it is usually phrased, and although this is a matter in which I thought it became me to be brief, I submit to you by telling you how it stood at the time of my leaving England. When I first discovered my inclinations, both Mary and I were so young that no one but myself considered the matter seriously, it serving no more than for tea-table talk amongst our friends. But afterwards, seeing the abiding nature of my passion, not the whit abated after two years, and which occasioned me to act without any regard to prudence or interest, or my father's consent, her parents began to consider it as a matter of consequence, and when I took my last leave of them, her mother, at the same time expressing the most tender affection for me as if I had been her own child, told me that though she had no objections to make that at a maturer age there should be a probability of our engaging upon a prudent prospect, yet as things then stood, she thought herself obliged to interfere, and therefore desired I would no more return to their house (unless Mary was from home) till such time as I could either prevail with myself entirely to give up my pretensions, or could assure her that I had my father's express consent to go on.

Much depended on Mary's part, and though she was young, gay, and quite unpractised in such matters, she was directed to a happy medium. She had penetration to see her absolute power over me, with the prudence to make a proper use of it and would neither understand my hints, nor give me room to come to a direct explanation. It was on these terms that we parted, although she has said since that from the first discovery of my regard, and long before the thought was agreeable to her, she had often an unaccountable impression that sooner or later she should be mine. So, while I had little satisfaction in my time with her, I was also sensible that I was taking pains to multiply my own troubles, as you will see presently happened. For the short time I could stay passed like a dream, and on New Year's Day, 1745, I took my leave to return to the ship.

The captain was prevailed on to excuse my absence, but this rash step (especially as it was not my first) highly displeased him, and lost me his favour, which I never recovered. At length we sailed from Spithead with a very large fleet. We put into Torbay with a change of wind, but it returning fair, we sailed again the next day. Several of our fleet were lost in attempting to leave that place, but the following night the whole fleet was greatly endangered upon the coast of Cornwall by a storm from southward, the darkness of the night and the number of the vessels occasioning much confusion and damage. Our ship, though several times in imminent danger of being run down, escaped unhurt, but many suffered much, particularly the admiral. This occasioned our putting back to Plymouth.

While we lay at Plymouth I heard that my father, who had interest in some of the ships lately lost, was come down to Torbay. He had a connection at that time with the African Company and I thought if I could get to him, he might easily introduce me into that service, which would be better than pursuing a long uncertain voyage to the East Indies. As it was a maxim with me in those days *never to deliberate*, the thought hardly occurred but I was resolved to leave the ship.

I did so, and in the wrongest manner possible. I was sent one day in the boat to take care that none of the crew deserted, but betrayed my trust and went off myself. I knew not what road to take, and durst not ask for fear of being suspected, yet having some general idea of the country, when I had travelled nine miles I found upon enquiry that I was on the road to Dartmouth. All went smoothly that day, and part of the next; I expected to have been with my father in about two hours, when I met a small party of soldiers. I could not avoid or deceive them. They brought me back to Plymouth; I walked through the streets guarded like a felon, my heart full of indignation, shame, and fear. I was confined two days in the guardhouse, then sent on board my ship, kept awhile in irons, then publicly stripped and whipped. After this I was degraded from my office, and all my former companions forbidden to show me the least favour, or even to speak to me. As midshipman I had been entitled to *some* command, which (being sufficiently haughty and vain) I had not been backward to exert. I was now, in my turn, brought down to a level with the lowest, and exposed to the ill will of all.

And if my present situation was uncomfortable, my future prospects were worse; the evils I suffered were likely to grow heavier every day. While my catastrophe was recent, the officers, my quondam brethren, were something disposed to screen me from ill usage, but during the little time I remained with them I found them cool very fast in their endeavours to protect me. Indeed they could not avoid it without the risk of sharing with me. For the captain, though in general a humane man to the ship's company, was almost implacable when he had been greatly offended, and took several occasions to show himself so to me. The voyage was expected to be (as it proved) for five years, yet nothing I either felt or feared distressed me as much as seeing myself forcibly torn away from the object of my affections, and under the great improbability of seeing her again. Thus I was as miserable as could be imagined. My breast was filled with the most excruciating passions: eager desire, bitter rage, and black despair. Every hour exposed me to some new insult and hardship, with no hope of relief or mitigation, no friend to take my part or listen to my complaint – nothing, inward or outward, but darkness and misery! I cannot express with what wishfulness and regret I cast my last looks upon the English shore; I kept my eyes fixed upon it, till the ship's distance increasing, it insensibly disappeared, and when I could see it no longer, I was tempted to throw myself into the sea, which (according to the wicked system I had adopted) would put a period to all my sorrows at once. But the secret hand of God retained me. Help me to praise him, dear sir, for his wonderful goodness to the most unworthy of all his creatures.

I am your most obliged servant.

15 January 1763

Letter IV

Dear Sir,

During our subsequent passage to Madeira, though I had well deserved all I met with, and the captain might well have been justified if he had carried his resentment still farther, yet my pride suggested that it was *I* that had been grossly injured, and this so far wrought upon my wicked heart, that I actually formed designs against his life – a reason that made me willing to prolong my own. I was sometimes divided between killing either him or myself, but could not discover a practicable means of effecting both. The Lord had now, to appearance, given me up and I was capable of anything. I had not the least fear of God, nor (so far as I remember) the least sensibility of conscience. I was possessed of such a strong a spirit of delusion as to believe my own lie, and yet some intervals of sober reflection would at times take place when a ray of hope would come in (though there was little probability for such a hope) that I should yet see better days, again return to England, and have my wishes crowned. In a word, my love for Mary Catlett was now the only restraint I had left. Though I neither feared God nor regarded men, I could not bear that *she* should think meanly of me if I should die. Thus I found this single thought, which had not restrained me from a thousand smaller evils, proved my only and effectual barrier against the greatest and most fatal temptations. How long I could have supported this conflict, or what would have been the consequence of my continuing in my then situation, I cannot say. But the Lord, whom I little thought of, knew my danger, and was providing for my deliverance.

Two things I had determined at Plymouth: that I would *not* go to India, and that I *would* go to Guinea, and such indeed was the Lord's will concerning me, but to be accomplished in his way, not in my own. We had been at Madeira some time and the fleet was to sail the following day. On that memorable morning I was late in bed, when a midshipman (an old companion) came down and, between jest and earnest, bid me rise. I did not immediately comply, and he cut down the hammock in which I lay, which forced me to dress myself. I was very angry, but durst not resent it – and was little aware how much his caprice was the messenger of God's Providence.

I said little, but went upon deck, where I that moment saw a man putting his clothes into a boat, who told me he was going to leave us. Upon inquiring, I was informed that two men from a Guinea ship, which lay near us, had been entered on board the *Harwich*, while the commodore (Sir George Pocock) had ordered the captain to send two others in their room. My heart instantly burned like fire. I begged the boat might be detained a few minutes; I ran to the lieutenants, and begged them to intercede with the captain that I, too, might be dismissed on this occasion. Though formerly upon ill terms with these officers, disobliging them all in turns, yet they now pitied my case, and were ready to serve me. The captain, who at Plymouth had refused to exchange me, though at the request of Admiral Medley, was now easily prevailed on. In a little more than half an hour from being asleep in bed, I saw myself discharged, and on board another ship: one of the many critical instances in my life, in which the Lord was pleased to display his Providence, by causing un-expected circumstances to concur in almost an instant of time; instances that were several times repeated, each of them bringing me into a new scene of action, and usually delayed to the last moment.

The ship I went on board, the *Pegasus*, was bound to Sierra Leone, and the adjacent parts of what is called the Windward Coast of Africa. The commander was a sometime acquaintance of my father who received me very kindly and, I believe, would have been my friend. But without heeding all former mistakes and troubles, I pursued the same courses, nay, if possible, much worse. On first going on board the *Harwich*, though my principles were totally corrupted, yet I was in some degree staid and serious. Now entering amongst strangers, I could appear without disguise; and I well remember, while I was passing from the one ship to the other, a reflection I made upon the occasion, viz., 'that I now might be as abandoned as I pleased'.

From this time I was exceedingly vile indeed, little short of that almost irrecoverable state we have in 2 Peter 2:14, that I not only sinned with a high hand myself, but made it my study to tempt and seduce others. One natural consequence of this was the loss of the favour of my new captain; not that he was at all religious, or disliked my wickedness any further than it affected his interest, but I became careless and disobedient. I did not please him because I did not intend it, and as he was a man of an odd temper likewise, we therefore more easily disagreed. Besides, I had a little of that unlucky wit, which only multiplies troubles and enemies to its possessor, and upon some imagined affront I made a song, in which I ridiculed his ship, his designs, and his person, and taught it to the whole ship's company. Such was the return I made for his offers of friendship and protection. I shall say no more of this part of my story; let it be buried in eternal silence.

This went on for about six months, by which time the ship was preparing to leave the African coast. A few days before she sailed the captain died. I was not upon much better terms with his mate, who now succeeded to the command, and had upon some occasion treated me ill. I had no doubt that if I went with him to the West Indies, he would put me on board a man-of-war and this, from what I had known already, was more dreadful to me than death. To avoid it, I determined to remain in Africa, and amused myself with many golden dreams that here I should find an opportunity of improving my fortune.

There are still upon that part of the coast a few white men settled (and were many more when I was first there), whose business it was to purchase slaves, etc., from adjacent rivers and country, and sell them to the ships at an advanced price. One of these had recently been in England and was returning in the vessel I was in, of which he owned a quarter part. This man, Clow, had initially landed in indigent circumstances like my own, but had since acquired considerable wealth. His example impressed me with hopes of similar success, and upon a condition of entering into his service I obtained my discharge. I did not take the precaution to make any terms regarding my employment, but trusted to his generosity. I received no compensation for my time on board the ship, but a wage bill upon the owners in England, which was never paid, for their firm failed before my return.

The day the vessel sailed, I landed upon the island of Benanoes, with little more than the clothes upon my back, as if I had escaped shipwreck.

I am, etc.

17 January 1763

3. I arrive at Africa and become a slave of slaves. After many trials and much suffering I am rescued.

Letter V

Dear Sir,

In the following two years, of which I am now to give some account, I was to have still deeper experience of the dreadful state of the heart of man when left to itself; I have seen frequent cause since, to admire the mercy of the Lord in banishing me to those distant parts, and almost excluding me from human society, at a time when I was big with mischief and, like one infected with a pestilence, was capable of spreading a taint wherever I went. Yet had my affairs taken a different turn, had I succeeded in my designs, and remained in England, my sad story would probably have been worse. But the Lord wisely placed me where I could do little harm. The few I had to converse with were much like myself, and I was soon brought into such abject circumstances, that I was too low to have any influence, being shunned and despised rather than imitated, there being few, even of the negroes themselves (during the first year of my residence among them) but thought themselves too good to speak to me.

It may not, perhaps, be amiss here to digress and give

you a very brief sketch of the geography of the circuit I
was now confined to, especially as I may have frequent
occasion to refer later to places I shall now mention, for
my trade afterwards, when the Lord gave me better
days, was chiefly to the same places, and with the same
persons – those by whom I had been considered as upon
a level with their meanest slaves.

From Cape de Verd, the most western point of Africa,
to Cape Mount, the whole coast is full of rivers; the
principal are Gambia, Rio Grande, Sierra Leone, and
Sherbro. Of the former, as it is well known, and I was
never there, I need say nothing. The Rio Grande (like
the Nile) divides into many branches near the sea. On
the most northerly, called Cacheo, the Portuguese have
a settlement. The most southern branch, known by the
name of Rio Nuna, is, or then was, the usual boundary
of the white men's trade northward. Sierra Leone is a
mountainous peninsula, uninhabited, and I believe
inaccessible upon account of the thick woods, excepting
those parts which lie near the water. The river is large
and navigable. From hence, about twelve leagues to the
south-east, are three contiguous islands, called the
Benanoes, about twenty miles in circuit: this was about
the centre of the white men's residence. Seven leagues
farther, the same way, lay the Plantanes, three small
islands, two miles distant from the continent at the
point, which form one side of the Sherbro. This river is
more properly a sound, running within a long island,

and receiving the confluence of several large 'rivers unknown to song', but far more deeply engraven in my remembrance than the Po or Tyber. The southernmost of these has a very peculiar course, almost parallel to the coast, so that in tracing it a great many leagues upwards, it will seldom lead one above three miles, and sometimes not more than half a mile from the seashore. Indeed I know not but that all these rivers may have communications with each other, and with the sea in many places. If you cast your eyes upon a large map of Africa, while you are reading this, you will have a general idea of the country I was in, for though the maps are very incorrect, most of the places I have mentioned are inserted, and in the same order as I have named them.

My new master, Clow, had formerly resided near Cape Mount, but now he settled at the Plantanes, upon the largest of the three islands. This is low, sandy, about two miles in circumference, and almost covered with palm trees. We immediately began to build a house, and began to trade. I had now some desire to retrieve my lost time, and to exert diligence, and he was a man with whom I might have lived tolerably well, if he had not been soon influenced by being under the direction of a black woman, who lived with him as a wife. A person of some consequence in her own country, Clow owed his first rise to her interest. This woman (I know not for what reason) was prejudiced against me from the first, and what made it worse for me was my being overtaken by a severe fit of illness which attacked me before I had opportunity to show what I could do in his service.

I was sick when he sailed in a shallop to Rio Nuna, and he left me in her hands. At first I was taken some care of, but not recovering soon, she grew weary and abandoned me, so that sometimes I could hardly procure a draught of cold water when burning with a fever. My bed was a mat spread upon a board, and a log of wood my pillow. When my fever left me, and my appetite returned, I would gladly have eaten, but there was little given unto me: although she lived in plenty herself, she hardly allowed me sufficient to sustain life, except now and then, when in the highest good humour, she would send me the scraps from her own plate after she had dined, and so greatly was my pride humbled I received these with thanks and eagerness, as the most needy beggar does alms.

Once, I remember, I was called to receive this bounty from her own hand, but being exceedingly weak, I dropped the plate. Those who live in plenty can hardly conceive how this loss touched me, but she had the cruelty to laugh at my disappointment; and though her table was still covered with dishes (for she lived in the European manner), she refused to give me any more. My distress has been at times so great, as to compel me to go by night, and pull up roots in the plantation (though at the risk of being punished as a thief), which

I have then eaten, raw, upon the spot, for fear of discovery. These roots are very wholesome food when boiled, but eaten raw are the same as if I had taken tartar emetic, so I often returned as empty as I went. Often I was relieved by strangers, nay, even by the slaves in chains, who secretly brought me victuals from their own slender pittance.

Next to pressing hunger, nothing is harder than scorn and contempt, and of this, too, I had an abundant measure. When I was very slowly recovering, she would sometimes pay me a visit – not to pity or relieve, but to insult me. She would call me worthless and indolent, and compel me to walk, which, when I could hardly do, she would set her attendants to mimic my motion, to clap their hands, laugh, and throw limes at me, or to throw stones. They were not only not rebuked, but all who depended on her favour must join in. Yet when she was out of sight, I was rather pitied than scorned by even the meanest of her slaves.

At length my master returned from his voyage; I complained of ill usage, but he would not believe me and, as I did it in her hearing, I fared no better for it. But on his second voyage he took me with him. We did pretty well for a while, till a brother-trader he met in the river persuaded him that I was unfaithful, and had stolen some of his goods in the night, or when he was on shore. This was almost the only vice I could not be charged with, the sole remnants of my good education being honesty, and though my great distress might, in some measure, have excused it, I never once thought of defrauding him. However, the charge was believed, and I was condemned without evidence.

So from that time he, likewise, used me very hardly. Whenever he left the vessel, I was locked upon deck, with a pint of rice for my day's allowance, and if he stayed overnight I had no relief till his return. Indeed, I believe I should have been nearly starved but for an opportunity of catching fish sometimes. When fowls were killed for his use, I seldom was allowed any part but the entrails with which to bait my hooks, and at slack water, that is, the changing of the tides, I used generally to fish (for at other times it was not practicable). If I saw a fish upon my hook, my joy was little less than any other person may have found in the accomplishment of the scheme he had most at heart. Such a fish, hastily broiled, or rather half burnt, without sauce, salt, or bread, has afforded me a delicious meal. If I caught none, I might (if I could) sleep away my hunger till the next slack water, and then try again. Now the rainy season was fast advancing, and as my whole suit was a shirt, a pair of trousers, a cotton handkerchief instead of a cap, and a cotton cloth, about two yards long, to supply the want of upper garments, I have been exposed for twenty, thirty, perhaps near forty hours together, in incessant rains, accompanied with strong gales of wind, without the least shelter, when my master was on shore, and often feel to this day some returns of the violent pains I then contracted. The excessive cold and wet I endured in that voyage, so soon after recovering from my long sickness, quite broke my constitution, and the effects remain with me as a memento of the service, and of the wages of sin.

In about two months we returned to adopt the same regimen at the Plantanes as I have already mentioned. My haughty heart was now brought low: not to a wholesome repentance or the language of the prodigal, but my spirits were quite sunk and I had lost all resolution, and almost all reflection. It seemed I had lost the fierceness which fired me when on board the *Harwich*, which made me capable of the most desperate attempts, but in reality I was no further changed than a tiger is tamed by hunger: remove the occasion, and he will be as wild as ever.

Had you seen me, sir, then go so pensive and solitary, in the dead of night, to wash my one shirt upon the rocks, and afterwards put it on wet, that it might dry upon my back while I slept; had you seen me so poor a figure, that when a ship's boat came to the island, shame often constrained me to hide myself in the woods from the sight of strangers; especially had you known that my conduct, principles, and heart were still darker than my outward condition, how little would you have imagined that one, who so fully answered to the 'hateful, and hating one another' of the apostle would be reserved to be so peculiar an instance of the providential care, and exuberant goodness of God.

One thing, though strange, is most true. Though destitute of food and clothing, and depressed beyond common wretchedness, I could sometimes collect my mind to mathematical studies. I had bought Barrow's *Euclid* at Plymouth, brought it on shore with me, and always had it by me. I used to take it to remote corners of the island by the seaside and, drawing my diagrams with a long stick upon the sand, I often beguiled away my sorrows, and almost forgot my feelings – and thus, without any other assistance, I made myself in a good measure, master of the first six books of *Euclid*.

I am,

Yours, as before.

17 January 1763

Letter VI

Dear Sir,

Looking back to some of those mournful days to which my last letter refers, I remember once I was busy plant-ing some lime or lemon trees when my master and his mistress passed by and stopped a while to look at me.

'Who knows', said he to me, 'but by the time these trees grow up and bear, you may go home to England, obtain the command of a ship, and return to reap the fruit of your labours.' This, as he intended it, was a cutting sarcasm and I believe he thought it full as probable that I should live to be king of Poland. Yet it proved a prediction, and they (one of them at least) lived to see me return from England in the capacity mentioned, and pluck some of the first limes from those very trees.

I know not exactly how long things continued with me thus, but I believe near a twelvemonth. In this interval I wrote two or three times to my father; I gave him an account of my condition, and desired his assistance, intimating at the same time that I had resolved not to return to England unless he was pleased to send for me. I have likewise letters wrote by me to Mrs Newton in that dismal period, so that at the lowest ebb it seems I still retained a hope of seeing her again.

I then obtained my master's consent to live with another trader who dwelt upon the same island, an alteration much to my advantage as I was soon decently clothed, lived in plenty, was considered as a companion, and trusted with the care of all his domestic effects, which were to the amount of some thousand pounds. This man had several factories, and white servants in different places, particularly one in Kittam, the river I spoke of which runs so near along the lee coast. I was soon appointed to go there, where I had a share in the management of business jointly with another of his servants. We lived as we pleased, business flourished, and our employer was satisfied. Here I began to be wretch enough to think myself happy.

There is a significant phrase frequently used in those parts, that such a white man is grown *black*. This does not intend an alteration of complexion, but disposition. I have known several who, settling in Africa after the age of thirty or forty, have at that time of life been gradually assimilated to the tempers, customs, and ceremonies of the natives so far as to prefer that country to England; they have even become dupes to all the pretended charms, necromancies, amulets, and divinations of the blinded negroes, and put more trust in such things than the wiser natives. A part of this spirit of infatuation was growing upon me (in time perhaps I might have yielded to the whole); I entered into closer engagements with the inhabitants, and should have lived and died amongst them, if the Lord had not been watching over me. Not that I had lost those ideas and thoughts of her who chiefly engaged my heart to England, but despair of ever seeing them accomplished made me willing to remain where I was.

In the meantime my father, having received my letters, applied to his friend, Mr Manesty, in Liverpool; who accordingly gave orders to a captain of his, who was then fitting out for the Gambia and Sierra Leone, to bring me home. This ship arrived at Sierra Leone: the captain made inquiry for me there, and at the Benanoes, but understanding that I was a great distance up country, he thought no more about me. Without doubt, the hand of God directed my being placed at Kittam just at this time; for as the ship came no nearer than the Benanoes, and stayed but a few days, if I had been at the Plantanes I would not have heard of her till she had sailed, the same applying had I been sent to any other factory, of which my new master had several upon different rivers. But though the place I was at was a long way up a river, yet by the peculiar parallel situation which I have already noticed, I was still within a mile of the sea coast. To make the interposition more remarkable, I was at that very juncture preparing to go in quest of trade a distance directly from the sea, and should have set out a day or two before, but that we decided to wait for a few articles from the next ship due to complete the assortment of goods I was to take with me.

We used then, sometimes, to walk on the beach, in expectation of seeing a vessel pass by, and in February 1747 (I know not the exact day) my fellow servant and I walking on the beach in the forenoon saw a vessel sailing past, and made a 'smoke' to signify we were ready to trade. She was already a little beyond us, and as the wind was fair, the captain was in some demur whether to stop or not; however, we saw her come to anchor and my companion went on board in a canoe. This was Mr Manesty's ship, the *Brownlow*, and the first question asked was concerning me, and when the captain understood I was so near he came on shore to deliver his message and a passage home. Had this reached me when I was sick and starving at the Plantanes I should have received it as life from the dead, but now, for the reasons already given, I heard it with indifference.

The captain, under orders and unwilling to lose me, then told me a story of his own framing, which he said he had heard from my father's own mouth, as well as from Mr Manesty's; that a person lately dead had left me £400 per annum, and that if I was presently any way embarrassed, he had express orders to redeem me though it should cost one half of his cargo. He claimed the proof of this was in a large packet of letters and papers he had somehow left behind. The captain further promised (and in this he kept his word) that I should lodge in his cabin, dine at his table, and be his constant companion – and without expecting any service from me.

Every particular regarding this inheritance was false, but as I had some expectations from an aged relation, I thought a part of it might be true. But though my father's care and desire to see me had too little weight with me, and would have been insufficient to make me quit my retreat, yet the remembrance of Mary, and the hopes that seeing her might once more put me in a way of gaining her hand, prevailed over all other con-siderations and I accepted the offer. And thus, suddenly freed from a captivity of about fifteen months that I had neither a thought nor a desire to change one hour previously, I embarked, and very shortly we lost all sight of Kittam.

How can I proceed in my relation till I raise a monument to the divine goodness with what I was at that time! How much are they to be pitied who can see nothing but chance in events of this sort! So blind and stupid was I at that time; I made no reflection, I sought no direction in what had happened: like a wave of the sea driven with the wind, and tossed, I was governed by present appearances, and looked no farther. But he, who is eyes to the blind, was leading me in a way that I knew not.

Believe me to be, with great respect,

Dear Sir,

Your affectionate and obliged servant.

18 January 1763

4. Returning to Liverpool the ship is caught in a great storm and we are on the brink of eternity. Here I find God. Supplies fail and cannibalism is in the air. I am seen as a Jonah to be thrown overboard. We finally make land.

Letter VII

Dear Sir,

The ship I was now on board as a passenger, the *Brownlow*, was on a trading voyage for gold, ivory, dyers-wood, and beeswax. A cargo of this sort requires much longer time to collect than that of slaves, and the captain, who had begun his trade at Gambia, had been already four or five months in Africa, and continued there a year more after I was with him. In this time we ranged the whole coast as far as Cape Lopez (o.6° S 7° E) which lies about a degree south of the equinoctial, and more than a thousand miles farther from England than the place where I embarked.

I have little to offer worthy your notice in the course of this tedious part of the voyage. Having no business to employ my thoughts, excepting at times a little mathematics, I instead applied myself to a course of the most horrid impiety and profaneness. I know not that I have ever since met so daring a blasphemer as myself for, not contenting with common oaths and imprecations, I daily invented new ones, so that I was often seriously reproved by the captain, even though he himself was a very passionate man, and not at all circumspect in his expressions. But although I lived long in the excess of almost every other extravagance, I never was fond of drinking, and my father was often heard to say that while I avoided drunkenness, he should still entertain hopes of my recovery. But sometimes I would promote a drinking bout, for a frolic sake, as I termed it, for though I did not love the liquor, I was bold to do iniquity, and delighted in mischief.

The last abominable frolic of this sort in which I was engaged was in the river Gabon, and both the proposal and expense were my own. Four or five of us one evening sat down upon deck, to see who could hold out longest in drinking Geneva and rum alternately, a large seashell supplying the place of a glass. Although I was unfit for a challenge of this sort, my head being always incapable of bearing much strong drink, it was I who began by proposing the first toast, which I well remember was some imprecation against the person who should start first: that is, myself. My brain was soon fired; I arose, and danced about the deck like a madman, and while I was thus diverting my companions, my hat went overboard. By the light of the moon I saw the ship's boat, and eagerly threw myself over the side to get into her, that I might recover my hat. In the circumstance I was in, my sight deceived me, for the boat was not within my reach, but perhaps twenty feet from the ship's side. I was, however, half overboard, and should in one moment more have plunged myself into the water, when somebody caught hold of my clothes and pulled me back. This was an amazing escape, as I could not swim while sober, much less drunk; the tide ran very strong; my companions were too much intoxicated to save me, and the rest of the ship's company were asleep. So near then was I to perishing and sinking into eternity under the weight of my own curse.

Another time, at Cape Lopez, some of us had been in the woods, and shot a buffalo, or wild cow. We brought a part of it on board, and carefully marked the place (as I thought) where we left the remainder. In the evening I undertook to be the guide and we returned to fetch it. But we set out too late, and night coming, we lost our way. Sometimes we were in swamps up to the middle in water, sometimes on dry land, but at no time could we tell whether we were walking towards the ship, or away from her, as we had no compass to form a judgement which way we were going, and so every further step increased our uncertainty. As the night grew even darker for the stars were now clouded, we became entangled in inextricable woods where, perhaps, the foot of man had never trod before. As well, that part of the country is entirely abandoned to wild beasts, with which it prodigiously abounds. We were indeed in a terrible case, having neither light, food, or arms, and expecting a tiger to rush from behind every tree. Had things continued thus, we had probably perished, but it pleased God to allow no beast near us, and after some hours of perplexity, the moon arose in the eastern quarter. It appeared then, that instead of drawing nearer to the seaside, we had been penetrating into the country, but by the guidance of the moon we at length came to the waterside, though a considerable distance from the ship. But eventually we got safe on board, without any other inconvenience than what we suffered from fear and fatigue. But this, and many other of God's deliverances, were at that time entirely lost upon me.

At length, our business finished, we left Cape Lopez and, after a few days at the island of Annabona to lay in provisions, we sailed homewards, about the beginning of January 1748. From Annabona to England, without touching at any intermediate port, is a very long navigation, perhaps more than seven thousand miles if we include the circuit necessary to be made on account of the trade winds. This circuit means that first we sail westward till near the coast of Brazil, then northwards, to the banks of Newfoundland. We reached these banks without meeting any thing extraordinary, and stopped there half a day to fish for cod. This was then chiefly for diversion as we thought we had provisions enough, and little expected those fish (as it afterwards proved) would be all we should have to subsist on for our survival. We left the banks on 1 March with a hard gale of wind westerly, which pushed us full homewards.

I should observe here, that with the length of time the ship had spent in such a very hot climate, the vessel was greatly out of repair, the sails and cordage were very much worn out, and the ship generally unfit to withstand stormy weather. Crossing east across the Atlantic we began to run into stormy weather and I think it was on 9 March (the day before our catastrophe) that I felt thoughts pass through my mind to which I had long been a stranger. Among the few books we had on board, one was Stanhope's *Thomas à Kempis*. I carelessly took it up, as I had often done before to pass away the time, but with the usual same indifference, as if it was entirely a romance. This time, however, an involuntary suggestion arose in my mind as regard its contents: what if these things be true? I could not bear the force of the inference as it related to myself and my own sins, and therefore quickly shut up the book. My conscience was witnessing against me once more, but I concluded that, true or false, I must abide the consequences of my own choice. I then put an abrupt end to these reflections by joining in with some vain conversation or other that came in the way.

But now the Lord's time was come, and those convictions I was so unwilling to acknowledge were shortly to be deeply impressed upon me by an awful dispensation. I went to bed that night in my usual security and indifference, but was suddenly awaked by the force of a violent sea breaking on board us. So much of it came below as to fill the cabin in which I lay with water. This was followed by a cry from the deck that the ship was going down. As soon as I could recover myself, I essayed to get up on deck but was met upon the ladder by the captain, who desired me to bring a knife with me. I turned back for the knife, and as I did so another person went up the ladder in my stead, to be instantly washed overboard.

We had no leisure to lament him, nor did we expect to survive him long, for we found the ship filling with water very fast. The sea had torn away the upper timbers on one side, the ship was filling, and we expected to be wrecked in a few minutes. We had immediate recourse to the pumps: while some of us were set to bailing in another part of the vessel, that is, to lade it out with buckets and pails. But as we had but eleven or twelve people to sustain this service, the water increased against all our efforts, and soon she was full, or very near it. With a common cargo she must have sunk, but we had a great quantity of beeswax and wood on board, specifically very lighter than the water, and as it pleased God, towards morning we were enabled to employ some means for our safety which succeeded beyond hope. We expended most of our clothes and bedding to stop the leaks (though the weather was exceeding cold, especially to us, who had so lately left a hot climate); over these we nailed pieces of boards, and at last perceived the water abate. At the beginning of this hurry I was little affected: I pumped hard, and endeavoured to animate myself and my companions. I told one of them, that in a few days this distress would serve us to talk of over a glass of wine, but he being a less hardened sinner than myself, replied with tears, 'No, it is too late now.'

In about an hour's time the day began to break, and the wind abated and at about nine o'clock, being almost spent with cold and labour, I went to speak with the captain, who was busied elsewhere, and just as I was returning from him, I said, almost without any meaning, 'If this will not do, the Lord have mercy on us.' This (though spoken with little reflection) was the first desire I had breathed for mercy in the space of many years. I was instantly struck with my own words, and as Jehu said once, 'What hast thou to do with peace?' so it directly occurred to me, 'What mercy can there be for me?'

I was obliged to return to the pump, and there I continued till noon, almost every passing wave breaking over my head, but we made ourselves fast with ropes, that we might not be washed away. Indeed, I expected that every time the vessel descended in the sea, she would rise no more, and though I dreaded death now, and my heart foreboded the worst if the Scriptures, which I had long since opposed, were indeed true. Yet I was still but half convinced, and so I remained for a space of time in a sullen frame, a mixture of despair and impatience. I thought, if the Christian religion was true I could not be forgiven, and was therefore expecting and almost, at times, wishing to know the worst of it.

I am, etc.

19 January 1763

Letter VIII

Dear Sir,

The tenth day of March 1748 is one much to be remembered by me, and I have never suffered it to pass wholly unnoticed since. For on that day the Lord sent for me from on high, and delivered me out of deep waters. I had continued at the pump from three in the morning till near noon and then, being able to do no more, went and lay down upon my bed, almost indifferent as to whether I should rise again. In an hour's time I was called and, not being able to pump, went to the helm and steered the ship till midnight, excepting a small interval for refreshment. At the wheel I had leisure and convenient opportunity for reflection and began to think of my former religious professions, the extraordinary turns in my life; the calls, warnings, and deliverances I had met with, the licentious course of my conversations; and, particularly, my unparalleled effrontery in making the Holy Scriptures the constant subject of profane ridicule. I thought there never was, nor could be, such a sinner as myself, and concluded at first that my sins were too great to be forgiven.

But as the day progressed, and I saw that beyond all probability there was still hope of respite, and heard about six in the evening that the ship was freed from water, there arose in me a gleam of hope and I thought I saw the hand of God displayed in our favour. I began to pray. I could not utter the prayer of faith, to draw near to a reconciled God, and call him Father. Rather, my prayer was like the cry of the ravens, which, even so, the Lord does not disdain to hear.

And now I began to think of Jesus, whom I had so often derided. I recollected the particulars of his life, and of his death; a death for sins not his own but, as I remembered, for the sake of those who in their distress should put their trust in him. But now, as I chiefly wanted evidence, the great question became – how to obtain *faith*, and gain an assurance that the Scriptures were of divine inspiration. One of the first helps I received (in consequence of a determination to examine the New Testament more carefully) was from Luke 9:13, 'If ye then, being evil, know how to give good gifts unto your children: how much more shall your heavenly Father give the Holy Spirit to them that ask him?' I had been sensible that to profess faith in Jesus Christ, when in reality I did not believe his history, was no better than a mockery of the heart-searching God, and thereby reasoned: if this book is true, the promise in this passage must be true likewise. I must therefore pray for that very spirit, by which the whole was wrote, in order to understand it aright, and if it is God, he will make good his words. My purposes were strengthened by John 7:17, 'If any man will do his will, he shall know of the doctrine, whether it be of God, or whether I speak of myself.'

I concluded from this, that though I could not say from my heart I believed the Gospel, yet I would for the present take it for granted, and that by studying it in this light I should be more and more confirmed in it. Our modern infidels would say (for I know too well their manner) that I was very desirous to persuade myself into this opinion. I was, and so would they be if the Lord should show them, as he showed me at that time, the necessity of some expedient to interpose between a righteous God and a sinful soul. So that at least on one side I saw hope, though on every other was surrounded with black unfathomable despair.

As the wind had now moderated, we began to recover from our consternation, though greatly alarmed by our circumstances. We found that the water having floated all our movables in the hold, all the cases of provisions had been beaten to pieces by the violent motion of the ship, while our livestock – such as pigs, sheep, and poultry – had been washed overboard. In effect, all our provisions, except for the fish I mentioned, would now scarce last us a week at short allowance. The sails, too, were mostly blown away, so that we advanced but slowly even while the wind was fair. We imagined ourselves about three hundred miles from land, but were, in reality, much further. Thus we proceeded slowly, with alternate hopes and fears, I now spending my leisure time reading and meditating on the Scripture, and praying to the Lord for mercy and instruction.

Things continued thus for four or five days till we were awakened one morning by the joyful shouts of the watch upon deck proclaiming the sight of land. We all soon congregated on deck; the dawning was un-commonly beautiful, and the light was just strong enough to discover the gladdening prospect of what seemed a mountainous coast, about twenty miles from us, that terminated in a cape or point with, a little further, two or three small islands rising out of the water. The appearance and position seemed exactly to resemble the north-west extremity of Ireland, to which we had been steering. We congratulated each other, having no doubt that if the wind continued we should be among safe and plenty the next day. The small remainder of our brandy (now little more than a pint) was, by the captain's orders, distributed amongst us, he adding at the same time, 'We shall soon have brandy enough.' We likewise ate up the residue of our bread and were like men suddenly reprieved from death.

But then the mate, with a grave tone, sunk our spirits by saying that he wished it might prove land. One of the common sailors saying this, I know not but the rest would have beat him, but the mate's grave warning brought on warm debates and disputes until the case was soon unanswerably decided by the day advancing fast, and our fancied islands growing red from the sun arising under them. In a word, our land was literally *in nubibus*, nothing but clouds, and in half an hour the whole disappeared.

Seamen often know deceptions of this sort; however, in this case, we comforted ourselves that the wind continuing fair, though we could not see the land yet, we should soon. But alas! That very day our fair wind subsided to a calm, and the next morning a gale sprung up from the south-east, directly against us, and continued for more than a fortnight afterwards. The ship was so wrecked, that we were obliged to keep the wind always on the broken side, and thus we were driven still further from our port, to the northward of all Ireland, as far as the Lewis or western islands of Scotland, a remote station which deprived us of any hope of being relieved by other vessels at that season of the year.

Provisions were now very short: the half of a salted cod was a day's subsistence for twelve people, and although we had plenty of fresh water, not a drop of stronger liquor, nor any bread, hardly any clothes, and very cold weather. We had incessant labour with the pumps and this, conjoined with little food, wasted us fast. One man died under the hardship. Yet our sufferings were light in comparison with our fears that soon we might be either starved to death, or reduced to feed upon one another. Our expectations grew darker every day, and I had a further trouble peculiar to myself.

The captain, whose temper was quite soured by distress, was hourly reproaching me (as I formerly observed) as the sole cause of the calamity, and was confident that if I was thrown overboard (and not otherwise), they should be preserved from death. He did not intend to make the experiment, but his continual repetitions gave me much uneasiness, especially as my conscience seconded his words, and I thought it probable that all that had befallen us was on my account, that I had at last been found out by the hand of God, and condemned in my own breast.

However, just as all was being given up for lost, and despair taking place in every countenance, I saw the wind come about to the very point we wished, blowing so gentle as our few remaining sails could bear, and thus continued, though at an unsettled time of the year, till we once more called up land – and this time it was land indeed. We saw the island, Tory, and the next day anchored in Lough Swilly in Ireland. This was 8 April 1748, and just four weeks after the damage we sustained from the sea. At this time our very last victuals were boiling in the pot, and before we had been there two hours the wind again began to blow with great violence, so that if we had continued at sea that night in our shattered, enfeebled condition, we must have gone to the bottom.

About this time I began to know that there is a providential God that hears and answers prayer, and how many times, since has he appeared for me since this great deliverance! Yet, alas! How distrustful and ungrateful is my heart even unto this hour!

I am, etc.

19 January 1763

5. I hear of my father's death but he leaves me his blessing for my marriage. I sign as mate on my first voyage proper on a slaver. I go to Chatham to make another proposal to my wife to be. I collect my first cargo of slaves and have a narrow escape from death.

Letter IX

Dear Sir,

I have brought my history down to the time of my arrival in Ireland in 1748. But before I proceed, I would look back a little, to give you some further account of the state of my mind, and how far I was helped against the inward difficulties which beset me, at a time when I had many outward hardships to struggle against. I had shared with the others hunger, cold, weariness, and the fears of sinking and starving; but, besides these, I felt a heart-bitterness that no one on board but myself had been in any way impressed with any sense of the hand of God – or, at least, not awakened to any concern for their souls. But also understand that no temporal dispensations can reach the heart, unless the Lord himself applies them. My companions in danger were either quite unaffected, or soon forgot it all, but it was not so with me: not because I was wiser or better than they, but because the Lord was pleased to vouchsafe me peculiar mercy – even though, before this, I hardened my neck still more and more after every reproof. I can see no reason why the Lord singled me out for mercy but this, 'that it seemed good to him', unless it was to show, by one astonishing instance, that with him 'nothing is impossible.'

The Lord had wrought a marvellous thing, and I was now no longer an infidel; I heartily renounced my former profaneness, was sorry for my past misspent life, and purposed an immediate reformation; I became quite freed from the habit of swearing, which seemed to have been deeply rooted in me as a second nature. Thus, to all appearance, I was a new man. From this period I could no more make a mock at sin, or jest with holy things. Therefore I consider this as the beginning of my return to God, or rather of his return to me; but I cannot consider myself to have been a believer (in the full sense of the word) till a considerable time afterwards.

I have told you that in the time of our distress we had fresh water in abundance, a considerable relief to us, as our spare diet was mostly salt fish without bread. We drank plentifully, and were not afraid of wanting water; yet our stock was much nearer to an end than we expected. We supposed that we had six large butts on board, and were safe arrived in Ireland before we discovered that five of them were empty, having been stoved by the violent agitation when the ship was full of water. If we had found this out while we were at sea, it would have greatly heightened our distress, as we must have drank more sparingly. Thus with souls mired in sin, drinking from the barrel of what seems an ever-overflowing well of infamies, while not realising how little such receptacles really hold.

While the ship was refitting at Lough Swilly, I repaired to Londonderry. I lodged at an exceeding good house, where I was treated with much kindness, and soon recruited my health and strength. I was now a serious professor of religion, went twice a day to the prayers at church, and determined to receive the sacrament the next opportunity. A few days before, I signified my intention to the minister, as the rubric directs, but I found this practice was grown obsolete. At length the day came; I arose very early, was very particular and earnest in my private devotion, and with the greatest solemnity engaged myself to be the Lord's for ever, and only his. This was not a formal, but a sincere surrender, under a warm sense of mercies recently received. That day I experienced a peace and satisfaction to which I had been hitherto a perfect stranger.

The next day I was abroad with the mayor of the city and some other gentlemen, shooting. Climbing a steep bank, I pulled my fowling-piece after me, holding it up in a perpendicular direction. It went off so near my face as to burn away the corner of my hat, which taught me that we are no less exposed to danger, even when we think ourselves in the greatest safety, than when all the elements seem conspiring to destroy us, and that Divine Providence is necessary both in utmost extremity, and our most peaceful situations.

During our stay in Ireland I wrote home. The *Brownlow* had not been heard of for eighteen months and had been given up for lost. My father had no expectation of hearing that I was alive, but he received my letter a few days before he left London. He went out as governor of York Fort in Hudson's Bay, from whence he never returned. I received two or three affectionate letters from him and he had intended to take me with him, but God designing otherwise, one thing or another delayed us in Ireland until it was too late. He sailed before I landed in England, but I never had the pleasure of seeing him more. I had hopes, three years later when he returned, I would have had the opportunity of asking his forgiveness for the uneasiness my disobedience had given him, but the ship that was to have brought him home came without him. According to the best accounts we received, he was seized with the cramp when bathing, and drowned.

But before his departure my father, willing to contribute all in his power to my satisfaction, paid a visit to my friends in Kent, and gave his consent to the union which had been so long talked of between Mary and myself. Thus when I returned to Chatham I found I had only the consent of one person to obtain, but with her I as yet stood at as great an uncertainty as on the first day I saw her.

I arrived at the latter end of May 1748, about the same day that my father sailed from the Nore, to find the Lord had provided me another father in the gentleman whose ship had brought me home – Mr Manesty. He received me with great tenderness, and the strongest expressions of friendship and assistance; and to him, as the instrument of God's goodness, I owe my all, for he immediately offered me the command of a ship. Upon mature consideration, I declined it for the present, as I thought I had better make another voyage first, and learn to obey, and acquire a further insight and experience in business, before venturing to undertake such a charge. The mate of the vessel I came home in was preferred to the command of a new ship, and I engaged to go in the station of mate with him. I made a short visit to London, etc., which did not fully answer my views, for although I had one opportunity of seeing Mary, I availed myself very little, for I was always exceeding awkward in pleading my own cause viva voce. But after my return to Liverpool, I put the question in such a manner, by letter, that she could not avoid (unless I had greatly mistaken her) to return me some sort of an explanation. Her answer (though penned with abundance of caution) satisfied me that she was free from any other engagement, and willing to wait the event of the voyage I was about to undertake. I should be ashamed to trouble you with these little details, if you had not yourself desired me.

I am, etc.

20 January 1763

Letter X

Dear Sir,

My connections with sea affairs have often led me to think that the varieties observable in Christian experience might well be illustrated from the circumstances of a voyage. Imagine to yourself a number of vessels, at different times, and from different places, bound to the same port; there are some things in which all these would agree – the compass steered by the port in view, the general rules of navigation, both as to the management of the vessel, and determining their astronomical observation, would be the same in all. In other respects they would differ: perhaps no two of them would meet with the same distribution of winds and weather. Some we see set out with a prosperous gale, and when they almost think their passage secured, they are checked by adverse blasts; and after enduring much hardship and danger, and frequent expectations of shipwreck, they just escape, and reach the desired haven. Others meet the greatest difficulties at first; they put forth in a storm, and are often beaten back; at length their voyage proves favourable, and they make port with a rich and abundant entrance. Some are hard beset with privateers and enemies, and obliged to fight their way through; others meet with little remarkable in their passage. Is it not thus in the spiritual life? Is it not similar with all true believers? The word of God is their compass, Jesus is both their polar star and their sun of righteousness; their hearts and faces are all set Sion-ward. Thus far they are as one; yet their experiences are far from uniform. Though all are exercised at times, yet some pass through the voyage of life much more smoothly than others. But he 'who walks upon the wings of the wind, and measures the waters in the hollow of his hand' will not suffer any of whom he has once taken charge to perish in the storms, though for a season, perhaps, many of them are ready to give up all hopes.

Therefore, we must not make the experience of others a rule to ourselves, nor our experiences a rule to others; yet these are common mistakes, and productive of many more. As to myself, every part of my case has been extraordinary; I have hardly met a single instance resembling it. Few, very few, have been recovered from such a dreadful state, and the few that have, have generally passed through the most severe convictions, and after the Lord has given them peace, their future lives have been usually more exemplary than common.

Now, as on the one hand my convictions were very

moderate, and far below what might have been expected from my dreadful past; so, on the other, my first beginnings in a religious course were as faint as can be well imagined. I never knew that season alluded to in Jer. 2:2, Rev. 2:4; usually called 'the time of the first love'. Who would *not* expect to hear after such a wonderful unhoped-for deliverance as I had received that I should not immediately cleave to the Lord with full purpose of heart, and consult no more with flesh and blood? But, alas! it was far otherwise with me. I had learned to pray; I set some value upon the word of God, and was no longer a libertine, but my soul still cleaved to the dust. Soon after my departure from Liverpool on the *Duke of Argyle* I began to intermit, and grow slack in waiting upon the Lord. I grew vain and trifling; and though my heart smote me often, my armour was gone, and I declined fast. By the time I arrived at Guinea, I seemed to have forgot all the Lord's mercies and was (profaneness excepted) almost as bad as before. The enemy prepared a train of temptations, I became his easy prey; and, for about a month, he lulled me asleep in a course of evil.

At length the Lord, whose mercies are infinite, interposed in my behalf. My business in this voyage, while upon the coast, was to sail from place to place in the longboat to purchase slaves. The ship was at Sierra Leone, and I then at the Plantanes, the scene of my former captivity, where every thing I saw should have reminded me of my present ingratitude. For I was now in easy circumstances, courted by those who formerly despised me: the lime trees I had planted were growing tall, and promised fruit the following year, against which time I now had expectations of fulfilling my old master's prophecy and returning with a ship of my own. But none of these things affected me till, at length, the Lord again interposed to save me by visiting me with a violent fever and once more brought me to myself. For I thought myself now summoned away; my past dangers and deliverances, my earnest prayers in the time of trouble, my solemn vows before the Lord, and my ungrateful returns for all his goodness, were all present to my mind at once and for a little while I concluded the door of hope to be quite shut. Weak, and almost delirious, I arose from my bed, and crept to a retired part of the island, and here I found a renewed liberty to pray. I durst make no more resolves, but cast myself before the Lord, to do with me as he should please, and I prayed to be enabled to hope and believe in a crucified Saviour.

The burden was removed from my conscience, and not only my peace, but my health was restored; I cannot say instantaneously, but I recovered from that hour, and so fast, that when I returned to the ship two days afterwards, I was perfectly well. And from that time I have been delivered from the power and dominion of sin, though as to the effects and conflicts of sin dwelling in me, I still 'groan, being burdened'. I now began again to wait upon the Lord; and though I have often grieved his spirit, and foolishly wandered from him (when, alas, shall I be more wise!), yet his powerful grace has hitherto preserved me from such black declensions as this last I recorded.

My leisure hours in this voyage were chiefly employed in relearning the Latin language. This desire took place from an imitation I had seen of one of Horace's Odes in a magazine. I began the attempt under the greatest disadvantages possible; for I had pitched upon perhaps the most difficult of the poets. I had picked up an old English translation of him, which, with Castalio's Latin Bible, were all my helps. I forgot a dictionary, but I would not therefore give up my purpose; and by comparing the Odes with the interpretation, and tracing the words, I could understand from one place to another by the index, and with what assistance I could get from the Latin Bible. In this way, by dint of hard industry, often waking when I might have slept, I made some progress before I returned, and not only understood the sense and meaning of many Odes, and some of the Epistles, but began to relish the beauties of the composition, and acquired a spice of what Mr Law calls classical enthusiasm. And indeed, by this means, I had Horace more *ad unguem* than some who are masters of the Latin tongue, for my helps were so few, that I generally had the passage fixed in my memory before I could fully understand its meaning.

My business in the longboat collecting slaves, during eight months we were upon the coast, exposed me to innumerable dangers and perils. From burning suns and chilling dews, winds, rains, and thunderstorms, in the open boat and, on shore, from long journeys through the woods, and the temper of the natives, who are in many places cruel, treacherous, and always watchful for opportunities for mischief. Several boats from other ships during that time were cut off; several white men poisoned, and from my own boat I buried six or seven people with fevers. When going on shore or returning from it in the little native canoes, I have been more than once or twice overset by the violence of the surf, or by a breach of the sea, and brought to land half dead (for I could not swim). An account of such escapes would swell to several sheets but I shall only select one instance, as a specimen of that wonderful Providence which watched over me for good, and which, I hope, you will think worthy of notice.

When our trade was finished, and we were near to sailing to the West Indies, the only remaining service I had to perform in the boat was to assist in bringing the wood for firing, and the drinking water, from the shore. We were then at Rio Sestors. I used to go into the river in the afternoon with the sea breeze, procure my loading in the evening, and return on board in the morning with the land wind. Several of these little voyages I had made, but the boat was grown old, and almost unfit for use. One day, having dined on board, I was preparing to return to the river as formerly; I had taken leave of the captain, received his orders, was ready in the boat, and just going to put off, that is, to let go our ropes, and sail from the ship. In that instant the captain came up from the cabin, and called me on board again. I went, expecting further orders; but he said, he had took it in his head (as he phrased it), that I should remain that day in the ship, and accordingly ordered another man to go in my stead. I was surprised at this, as the boat had never been sent away without me before, and asked him the reason; he could give me no reason but as above, that so he would have it.

Accordingly the boat went without me, but returned no more. She sunk that night in the river, and the person who had supplied my place was drowned. I was much struck when we received news next morning. The captain himself, though quite a stranger to religion, so far as to deny a particular Providence, could not help being affected, but still declaring he had no other reason for countermanding me at that time, but that it came suddenly into his mind. Since, I have always thought it one of the most extraordinary circumstances of my life.

I am, etc.

21 January 1763

6. We sell the slaves at Charleston, Carolina, and I meet and talk with serious professors of religion. We sail back to Liverpool. I go to Chatham and am married to Mary Catlett. I sail again from Liverpool as captain of the *African*. I study Latin and theology during the voyage and return safely home. I sail again as captain in 1752. My men mutiny as do the slaves. I quell both uprisings. My days are eight hours for sleep and meals, eight hours for exercise and devotion, and eight hours to my books. At Antigua my wife's letters go astray and I think I am suffering from a broken heart. The letters arrive. I return to Liverpool.

Letter XI

Dear Sir,
A few days after I was thus wonderfully saved from this danger, we sailed for Antigua, and thence to Charles-town in South Carolina. In this place there are many serious religious people, but I knew not where to find them out. Indeed, I was not aware of a difference, but supposed that all who attended public worship were good Christians. I was as much in the dark about preaching, not doubting but whatever came from the pulpit must be very good. I had two or three

opportunities of hearing a dissenting minister named Smith, who, by what I have known since, I believe to have been an excellent and powerful preacher of the gospel, but I did not rightly understand him. The best words that men can speak are ineffectual till explained by the spirit of God.

Yet even brought to grace and reflection, my conduct was now very inconsistent. Almost every day, when business would permit, I used to retire into the woods and fields (for these, when at hand, have always been my favourite oratories) and here began to taste the sweets of communion with God in the exercises of prayer and praise. Yet I *still* frequently spent the evenings in vain and worthless company. Now, however, my relish for worldly diversions was much weakened, and I was rather a spectator than a sharer, but did not as yet see the necessity of an absolute forbearance. Indeed, I came to understand my compliance with custom and company was chiefly owing to want of light, rather than to an obstinate attachment to such pleasures; and as the Lord was pleased to preserve me from what I *knew* was sinful, I had for the most part peace of conscience. As yet I knew not the force of that precept, 'Abstain from all appearance of evil', but although I very often ventured upon the brink of temptation the Lord was gracious to my weakness, and would not suffer the enemy to prevail against me.

We finished our voyage, and arrived back in

Liverpool. When the ship's affairs were settled I went
to London, and from thence (as you may suppose) I
soon repaired to Kent. More than seven years had
elapsed since my first visit, but I felt every obstacle was
now removed. I had renounced my former follies, my
interest was established, and friends on all sides
consenting: the point was now entirely between ourselves, and, after what had passed was easily concluded.
Accordingly, our hands were joined on 1 February 1750.

The satisfaction I have found in this union you will
suppose has been greatly heightened by reflection on
the former disagreeable setbacks I had passed through,
and the views I have had of the singular mercy and
providence of the Lord in bringing it to pass. If you
please to look back to my sixth letter, I doubt not but
you will allow that few persons have known more of
either the misery or happiness of which human life is
capable. How easily, at a time of life (but a few months
more than seventeen) might my affections have been
fixed where they could have met with no return, or
where success would have been the heaviest disappointment. The long delay I met with was indeed a
mercy; for had I succeeded a year or two sooner, before
the Lord was pleased to change my heart, we must have
been mutually unhappy, even to the present day.

But, alas, I soon began to feel that my heart was
still hard and ungrateful to the God of my life. This
crowning mercy, my marriage, which raised me to

all I could wish in the temporal view, and which ought to have been the animating motive to obedience and praise, had a contrary effect. I rested in the gift, and forgot the giver. My poor narrow heart was now *satisfied*, and a cold carelessness to spiritual things grew daily.

Happy for me, the season was advancing, and in June I received orders to repair to Liverpool. This roused me from my dream, although I need not tell you that I found the pains of absence and separation fully proportionate to my preceding pleasure. It was hard, very hard, to part, especially as conscience interfered, and suggested to me how little I deserved that we should be spared to meet again. But I now had acquaintance with the way of access to a throne of grace by the blood of Jesus, and peace was soon restored to my conscience.

While I remained in England, we corresponded every post; and all the time I was at sea afterwards, I constantly kept up the practice of writing two or three times a week (if weather and business permitted), even though no conveyance homeward might offer for six or eight months together. My packets (letters) were usually heavy, and as not one of them at any time miscarried, I have to the amount of near two hundred sheets of paper now lying in my bureau of that correspondence. I mention this little relief I contrived to soften the intervals of absence, because it had a good effect beyond my first intention. It habituated me to think and write upon a great variety of subjects, and to acquire a greater readiness of expressing myself than I should have otherwise attained. As I gained more ground in religious knowledge, my letters became more serious, and at times I still find an advantage in looking them over, especially as they remind me of many providential incidents, and the state of my mind at different periods in these voyages, which would otherwise escape my memory.

I sailed from Liverpool in August 1750, commander of a good ship – the *African*. I have no very extraordinary events to recount from this period, and shall therefore contract my memoirs lest I become tedious. I had now the command and care of thirty persons; I endeavoured to treat them with humanity, and to set them a good example; I likewise established public worship, according to the liturgy, twice every Lord's day, officiating myself. Farther than this I did not proceed while I continued in that employment.

As captain, having now much more leisure, I prosecuted the study of Latin with good success. I brought out with me a dictionary this voyage, and procured two or three other books, but still it was my luck to choose the hardest. I added Juvenal to Horace, and for prose authors, I pitched upon Livy, Caesar, and Sallust. You will easily conceive, sir, that I had hard work to begin (where I should have left off) with Horace and Livy. I was not aware of the difference of style; I had heard Livy highly commended, and was resolved to understand him. I began with the first page, and laid down a rule, which I seldom departed from, not to proceed to a second period till I understood the first, and so on. I was often at a stand, but seldom discouraged; here and there I found a few lines quite obstinate, and was forced to break in upon my rule, and give in to them. But there were not many such, for before the close of that voyage, I could (with a few exceptions) read Livy from end to end, almost as readily as an English author. And I found, in surmounting this difficulty, I had surmounted all in one.

Other prose authors, when they came my way, cost me little trouble. In short, in the space of two or three voyages, I became tolerably acquainted with the best classics and at length conceived a design of becoming Ciceronian myself, and thought it would be a fine thing indeed to write pure and elegant Latin. I made some essays towards it, but by this time the Lord was pleased to draw me nearer to himself, and to give me a fuller view of the inestimable treasure hid in the field of the Holy Scripture; and for the sake of this I parted with all my new acquired riches as neither poet or historian could tell me a word of Jesus; so I therefore applied myself to those who could. I have not looked in Livy these five years, and suppose I could not now well understand him. Some passages in Horace and Virgil I still admire, but they seldom come in my way, and I prefer Buchanan's psalms to a whole shelf of Elzevirs.

About the same time, and for the same reasons, I laid aside the mathematics. I found they not only cost me much time, but engrossed my thoughts too far; my head was literally full of *schemes.* I became weary of cold, contemplative truths, which can neither warm nor amend the heart, but rather tend to aggrandize *self.* I do not regret that I have had opportunities of knowing the first principles of these things, but praise the Lord that he inclined me to stop in time. Whilst I was 'spending my labours for that which is not bread', he was pleased to set before me 'wine and milk without money and without price'.

My first voyage was fourteen months, through various scenes of danger and difficulty, but nothing very remarkable; and, as I intend to be more particular with regard to the second, I shall only say that I was preserved from every harm, and having seen many fall on my right hand and on my left, I was brought home in peace, and restored to where my thoughts had been often directed, 2 November 1751.

I am, etc.

22 *January 1763*

Letter XII

Dear Sir,

I almost wish I could recall my last sheet, and retract my promise. I seem to have engaged too far, and shall prove a mere egotist. What have I more that can deserve your notice ? However, I believe you will have candour to excuse what nothing but a sense of your kindness could extort from me.

Soon after the period where my last closes, that is, in the interval between my first and second voyage after my marriage, I began to keep a sort of diary, a practice which I have since found of great use. I had in this interval repeated proofs of the ingratitude and evil of my heart. A life of ease, in the midst of my friends, and the full satisfaction of my wishes, was not favourable to the progress of grace, and afforded cause of daily humiliation. Yet, upon the whole, I gained ground to become acquainted with books which gave me a farther view of Christian doctrine and experience, particularly, Scougal's *Life of God in the Soul of Man*, and Hervey's *Meditations.* As to preaching, I heard none but the common sort, and had hardly an idea of any better, not having the advantage of many Christian acquaintances. I was likewise greatly hindered by a cowardliness in that I was afraid of being thought precise. And though I could not live without prayer, I durst not propose it even to my wife, till she herself first suggested it – so far was I from those expressions of zeal and love so suitable to the case of one who had been much forgiven.

However, in a few months the returning season called me abroad again, and I sailed from Liverpool in a new ship in July 1752. A seafaring life is necessarily excluded from the benefits of attending public divine services and Christian communion. In other respects, I know not any calling that seems more favourable, or affords greater advantages to an awakened mind, for promoting the life of God in the soul, especially to a person who has the command of a ship, and thereby has it in his power to restrain gross irregularities in others, and to dispose of his own time. This is still more so in African voyages, as these ships carry a double proportion of men and officers to most others, which made my department very easy; and, excepting the hurry of trade, collecting slaves, etc., upon the coast, which is rather occasional than constant, afforded me abundance of leisure.

To be at sea in these circumstances, withdrawn out of the reach of innumerable temptations, with opportunity and a turn of mind disposed to observe the wonders of God in the deep, with the two noblest objects of sight, the expanded heavens, and the expanded ocean continually in view; these are helps to quicken and confirm the life of faith, which, in a good measure, supply to a religious sailor the want of those advantages which can be only enjoyed upon the shore. Indeed, though my knowledge of spiritual things (as knowledge is usually estimated) was at this time very small, yet I sometimes look back with regret upon those scenes. I never knew sweeter or more frequent hours of divine communion than in my two last voyages to Guinea, when I was either almost secluded from society on shipboard, or when on shore amongst the natives. I have wandered through the woods, reflecting on the singular goodness of the Lord to me, in a place where, perhaps, there was not a person that knew him for some thousand miles round me. Many a time, upon these occasions, I have restored the beautiful lines of Propertius to their right owner, lines full of blasphemy and madness, when addressed to a creature, but full of comfort and propriety in the mouth of a believer.

> In desert woods with thee, my God,
> Where human footsteps never trod,
> How happy could I be !
> Thou my repose from care, my light
> Amidst the darkness of the night,
> In solitude, my company.

In the course of this voyage I was wonderfully preserved in the midst of many obvious and many unforeseen dangers. At one time there was a conspiracy amongst my own people to turn pirates, and take the ship from me. When the plot was nearly ripe, and they only waited a convenient opportunity, two of those concerned in it were taken ill one day; one of them died, and he was the only person I buried while on board. This suspended the affair, and opened a way to its discovery, or the consequence might have been fatal.

The slaves on board were likewise frequently plotting insurrections, and were sometimes upon the very brink of mischief, but it was always disclosed in due time. When I have thought myself most secure, I have been suddenly alarmed with danger, and when I have almost despaired of life, as sudden a deliverance has been vouchsafed me. My stay upon the coast was long, the trade very precarious, and in the pursuit of my business, both on board and on more, I was *near death often*. Let the following instance serve as a specimen.

I was at a place called Mana, near Cape Mount, where I had transacted very large concerns with slaves, and had, at the time I am speaking of, some debts and accounts to settle, which required my attendance on shore. I intended to go there the next morning. Accordingly, when I arose I left the ship, but when I came near the shore, the surf, or breach of the sea, ran so high, that I was almost afraid to attempt landing. Indeed I had often ventured at a worse time, but I felt an inward hindrance and backwardness, for which I could not account. The surf furnished a pretext for indulging it and not landing, and after waiting and hesitating for about half an hour, I returned to the ship, without doing my business. Except for that morning, in all the time I used the trade, I never failed to go ashore to complete business. But I soon perceived the reason of all this: it seems, the day before I intended to land, a scandalous and groundless charge had been laid against me (by whose instigation I could never learn), which greatly threatened my honour and interest both in

Africa and England, and would perhaps have affected my life if I had landed according to my intention. I shall perhaps enclose a letter, which will give a full account of this strange adventure, and therefore shall say no more of it here, rather than to tell you that this attempt, aimed to destroy either my life or character, passed off without the least inconvenience. The person most concerned owed me about a hundred pounds, which he sent me in a huff, and otherwise perhaps would not have paid me at all. I was very uneasy for a few hours, but was soon afterwards comforted. I heard no more of my accusation till the next voyage, and then it was publicly acknowledged to be a malicious calumny, without the least shadow of a ground.

Such were some of the vicissitudes and difficulties through which the Lord preserved me. Now and then both faith and patience were sharply exercised, but suitable strength was given me. As to my time, in this I was very regular in its management. Every day I allotted eight hours for sleep and meals, eight hours for exercise and devotion, and eight hours to my books, and thus, by diversifying my engagements, the whole day was agreeably filled up, and I seldom found one too long, or had an hour to spare.

From the coast I went to St Christopher's, and here my idolatrous heart was its own punishment. The letters I expected from Mrs Newton were, by mistake, forwarded to Antigua, which had been at first proposed as our port. As I was certain of her punctuality in writing, if alive, I concluded, by not hearing from her, that she was surely dead, a fear which gradually began to affect me more and more. I lost my appetite and rest; I felt an incessant pain in my stomach, and in about three weeks I was near sinking under the weight of an imaginary stroke. I felt some severe symptoms of that mixture of pride and madness which is commonly called a broken heart, and indeed I wonder that this case is not more common than it appears to be. My complaint, however, was not all grief; conscience had a share. I thought my unfaithfulness to God had deprived me of her, especially my backwardness in speaking to her of spiritual things, which I could hardly attempt, even to her.

It was this thought, that I had lost invaluable, irrecoverable opportunities, to which both duty and affection should have driven me, that chiefly stung me, and I would have given the world to know she was living (that I might at least discharge my engagements by writing), though I should never see her again. This was a sharp lesson, but I hope it did me good, and when I had thus suffered some weeks, I thought of sending a small vessel to Antigua. I did so, and she returned bearing me several packets, which restored my health and peace, and gave me a strong contrast of the Lord's goodness to me, and my unbelief and ingratitude towards him.

In August 1753 I returned to Liverpool. My stay was very short at home that voyage, only six weeks, in which space nothing very memorable occurred; I shall therefore begin my next with an account of my third and last voyage. And thus I give both you and myself hopes of a speedy end to these memoirs, which begin to be tedious and minute even to myself, and am only still animated by the thought that I write at your request, and have therefore an opportunity of showing something of myself.

I am, etc.

31 January 1763

7. My third voyage. I take an old friend who proves a libertine. I leave him on the African coast where he dies of his excesses. At St Kitts I meet as serious a fellow Christian as myself. Back at Liverpool preparing for my next voyage in November, 1754, I am visited with an apoplectic stroke and my sea career is ended. Mrs Newton now falls very ill. I am fortunate to be appointed Tide Surveyor to Liverpool and begin to prepare myself to enter the Church of England ministry.

Letter XIII

Dear Sir,

My third voyage was shorter and less perplexed than either of the former. Before I sailed, I met with a young man who had formerly been a midshipman, and my intimate companion on board the *Harwich*. He was, at the time I first knew him, a sober youth, but I found too much success in my unhappy attempts to infect him with libertine principles. When we met at Liverpool, our acquaintance was renewed upon the ground of our former intimacy. Our conversation frequently turned upon religion, and I was very desirous to repair the mischief I had done him. I gave him a plain account of the manner and reason of my change, and used every argument to persuade him to relinquish his infidel schemes; and when I sometimes pressed him so close that he had no other reply to make, he would remind me that I was the very first person who had given him an idea of his liberty. This occasioned me many mournful reflections.

He was himself going as master to Guinea, but before his ship was ready, his owner became a bankrupt and his voyage was cancelled. As he had no further expectations, I offered to take him as a companion, that he might gain a knowledge of the coast, while the gentleman who employed me, Mr Manesty, promised to provide for him upon his return. My object in all this was not so much to serve him in business, but to have the opportunity of debating with him at leisure, in the hope that in the course of the voyage, my arguments, example, and prayers, might have some good effect on him. However, my intentions proved better than my judgement, and I had frequent reason to repent it. He was exceedingly profane, and while I saw in him a most lively picture of what I had once been, it was very inconvenient to have it always before my eyes. Besides, not only was he deaf to my remonstrances himself, but laboured all he could to counteract my influence upon others, while his spirit and passions required all my prudence and authority to hold him in any degree of restraint. He was as a sharp thorn in my side for some time, but at length I had an opportunity upon the coast of buying a small vessel which I supplied with a cargo from my own ship, and giving him command of this second ship, I sent him away to trade on the owner's account. When we parted, I repeated and enforced my best advice and he seemed greatly affected. But my words had no weight with him. Once he found himself from under my eye he gave loose to every appetite, and his violent irregularities, joined to the heat of the climate, soon threw him into a malignant fever, which carried him off in a few days. The account I had from those who were with him was dreadful; his rage and despair struck them all with horror, and he pronounced his own fatal doom before he expired, without any appearance that he either *hoped* or *asked* for mercy.

I left the coast after about four months, and sailed for St Christopher's. Hitherto I had enjoyed a perfect state of health in every climate for several years, but upon this passage I was visited with a fever, which gave me a very near prospect of eternity. Although I had not that full assurance which is so desirable at a time when flesh and heart fails, still, my hopes were greater than my fears, and I felt a silent composure of spirit, which enabled me to wait the event without much anxiety; the words 'he is able to save to the uttermost' gave me great relief. I was, for a while, troubled with a very singular thought: I seemed not so much afraid of wrath and punishment, as of being lost and overlooked amidst the myriads of souls that are continually entering the unseen world. What is mine (thought I), amongst such an innumerable multitude of beings. Perhaps the Lord will take no notice of me, but then a text of scripture, very apposite, occurred to my mind. 'The Lord knoweth them that are his.' In about ten days, to the surprise of those about me, I began to mend, and by the time of our arrival in the West Indies I was perfectly recovered.

Thus far, that is, for about the space of six years, the Lord was pleased to lead me in a secret way. I had learned something of the evil of my heart; I had read the Bible over and over, and had a general view of the gospel truth, but my conceptions were, in many respects, confused, not having in all this time met with one acquaintance who could assist my inquiries. But upon my arrival at St Christopher's, I found a captain of a London ship, a member of Mr B—r's church, and a man of experience in the things of God, and of a lively communicative turn. We discovered each other by some casual expressions in mixed company, and soon became (as far as business would permit) inseparable. For near a month we spent every evening together on board each other's ship alternately, often prolonging our visits till daybreak. I was all ears, and he not only informed my understanding, but also inflamed my heart. He encouraged me to open my mouth in social prayer; taught me the advantage of Christian converse; he put me upon an attempt to make my profession more public and to venture to speak for God. From him, or rather from the Lord by his means, I received an increase of knowledge, and I was delivered from the fear of relapse. He likewise gave me a general view of the state of religion, with the errors and controversies of the times (things to which I had been entirely a stranger), and finally directed me where to apply in London for further instruction. With these newly-acquired advantages my seven week passage homewards gave me leisure to digest what I had received; I had much comfort and freedom, and my sun was seldom clouded. I arrived safe in Liverpool, August 1754.

My stay at home was intended to be short, and by the beginning of November I was again ready for the sea, but the Lord saw fit to overrule my design. During the time I was engaged in the slave trade, I never had the least scruple as to its lawfulness, and was, upon the whole, satisfied that it was the work Providence had marked out for me. It is indeed accounted a genteel employment, and is usually very profitable, though to me it did not prove so, the Lord seeing that a large increase of wealth would not be good for me. However, it is true I was a sort of gaoler or turnkey, and I was sometimes shocked with an employment that was perpetually conversant with chains, bolts, and shackles. In this view, I had often petitioned in my prayers that the Lord (in his own time) might fix me in a more humane calling, and (if it might be) place me where I might have more frequent converse with his people and ordinances, and be freed from those long separations from home, which were very hard to bear. My prayers were now answered, though in a way I little expected. I was within two days of sailing, and to all appearance in good health as usual; but in the afternoon, as I was sitting with Mrs Newton drinking tea and talking over past events, I was in a moment seized with a fit – I suppose it was of the apoplectic kind – which deprived me of sense and motion, and left me without sign of life. It lasted about an hour, and when I recovered, it left such a pain and dizziness in my head that the physicians judged it would not be safe or prudent for me to proceed on the voyage. Accordingly, by the advice of Mr Manesty, to whom the ship belonged, I resigned my command, and was thereby freed from the future consequences of that voyage, which proved extremely calamitous, as the person who replaced me, most of the officers, and many of the crew, died and the vessel was brought home with great difficulty.

As I was now disengaged from business, I left Liverpool, and spent most of the following year at London and in Kent. But I entered upon a new trial. You will easily conceive that Mrs Newton was present while I lay, as she thought, expiring upon the ground. In effect, the blow that struck me reached her in the same instant. She did not immediately feel it, till her apprehensions on *my* account began to subside but as I grew better, she became worse, and she was thrown into a disorder which no physicians could define. Without any of the ordinary symptoms of a consumption, she decayed almost visibly, till she became so weak that she could hardly bear anyone to walk across the room she was in. I was placed for about eleven months in what Dr Young calls the 'dreadful post of observation, darker every hour'.

It was not till after my settlement in my present station, Tide Surveyor here at Liverpool, that the Lord was pleased to restore her by his own hand, when all hopes from ordinary means were at an end. But before this took place, I have some other particulars to mention, which must be the subject of the following sheet, which I hope will be the last on this subject.

I am, etc.

1 February 1763

Letter XIV

Dear Sir,

By the directions I had received from my friend at St Kitts, I soon found out the religious acquaintance he recommended in London. I first applied to Mr B and from him received many helps, both in public and private, for he was pleased to favour me with his friendship. His kindness, and the intimacy between us, has continued and increased to this day, and of all my many friends, I am most deeply indebted to him. The late

Mr H—d was my second acquaintance, a man of a choice spirit, and with an abundant zeal for the Lord's service. I enjoyed his correspondence till near the time of his death. Soon after, upon Mr W—d's return from America, my two good friends introduced me to him, and though I had little personal acquaintance with him till afterwards, his ministry was exceeding useful to me. I had likewise access to some religious societies, and became known to many excellent Christians in private life. Thus, when at London, I lived at the fountain-head, as it were, for spiritual advantages. When I was in Kent it was very different, yet I found some serious persons there, but the fine variegated woodland country afforded me advantages of another kind. Most of my time, at least some hours every day when the weather was fair was spent in retirement – sometimes in the thickest woods, sometimes on the highest hills. It has been my custom, for many years, to perform my devotional exercises in the open air when I have opportunity, as I find rural scenes have some tendency both to refresh and to compose my spirits. When I am withdrawn from the noise and petty works of men, I consider myself as in the great temple which the Lord has built for his own honour.

The country between Rochester and Maidstone, bordering upon the Medway, was well suited to the turn of my mind, and was I to go over it now, I could point to many a place where I remember to have either earnestly sought, or happily found, the Lord's presence with my soul. So I lived sometimes at London, and sometimes in the country, till the autumn of the following year. All this while I had two trials on my mind. The first, and principal, was Mrs Newton's illness. She still grew worse, and I had daily more reason to fear that the hour of separation was at hand, and although I was in some measure resigned to the Lord's will, too often my heart rebelled, and I found it hard either to trust or to submit. My second care was about my future settlement. The African trade was overdone that year, and my friends did not care to fit out another ship till mine returned. I was for some time in suspense, but trusted in the Lord, and accordingly was answered when, in August, I received an account that I was nominated to the office of Tide Surveyor at Liverpool. These places are usually obtained, or at least sought, by dint of much interest and application, but this came to me unsought and unexpected.

I knew, indeed, my good friend in Liverpool had endeavoured to procure another post for me, but found it pre-engaged. I found afterwards, that the place I had missed would have been very unsuitable for me, and that this, which I had no thought of, was the very thing I could have wished for as it afforded me much leisure, and the liberty of living in my own way.

But while I gained this point, my distress as regards Mrs Newton was doubled; I was obliged to leave her in the greatest extremity of pain and illness, with the physicians declaring they could do no more, and with no grounds of hope that I should ever see her again alive – except for the fact that nothing is impossible with the Lord. I had a severe conflict about leaving her, but faith prevailed, and the day before I set out, and not till then, the burden was entirely taken from my mind. I was strengthened to resign both her and myself to the Lord's disposal, and departed from her in a cheerful frame. Soon after I was gone she began to recover so fast that in two months I had the pleasure to meet her at Stone, on her journey to Liverpool.

And now I hope I have answered, if not exceeded, your desire. Since October 1755, we have been comfortably settled here, in remarkably smooth and uniform circumstances. My trials have been light and few, the principal one being the body of sin and death, which makes me often to sigh out the apostle's complaint, 'O wretched man!' but with him likewise I can say, 'I thank God through Jesus Christ my Lord.' I live in a barren land, where the knowledge and power of the gospel is very low, yet even in this wilderness there are a few of the Lord's people, and it has proved a useful school where I have studied more leisurely the truths I gathered up in London, though we can receive no knowledge further than he is pleased to communicate.

Since the year 1757, I have had an increasing acquaintance in the West Riding of Yorkshire, where the gospel flourishes greatly. This has been a good school to me where I have conversed at large among all parties, without joining any, and in my attempts to hit the golden mean, I have sometimes been drawn too near the different extremes, yet the Lord has enabled me to profit by my mistakes. In brief, I am still a learner, and the Lord still condescends to teach me, and I trust in him to carry on his own work in my soul, and to increase my knowledge of him, and of myself.

When I was fixed in a house in Liverpool, and found my business afforded me much leisure time, I considered in what manner I should use this time, and closing with the apostle's determination, 'to know nothing but Jesus Christ and him crucified', decided to devote my life to the prosecution of spiritual knowledge. This resolution divorced me (as I have already stated) from the classics and mathematics. But now my first attempt was to learn enough Greek as would enable me to understand the New Testament and Septuagint, and when I had made some progress this way, to enter on Hebrew the next year, and two years afterwards I began Syriac. You must not think that I have attained a critical skill in any of these; I had no business with them, but as in reference to something else. I only wanted the signification of scriptural words and phrases and now, in the Hebrew, I can read the historical books and psalms with tolerable ease, but in the prophetical and difficult parts, I am frequently obliged to have recourse to lexicons, etc. However, I know so much, as to be able with such helps as are at hand to judge for myself the meaning of any passage I have occasion to consult. Beyond this I do not think of proceeding, for I would rather be some way useful to others, than die with the reputation of an eminent linguist.

Together with these studies, I have kept up a course of reading of the best writers in divinity that have come to my hand in the Latin and English tongues, and some French (for I picked up the French while I used the sea). But within these two or three years, I have accustomed myself chiefly to writing, and have not found time to read much besides the Scriptures. I am the more particular in this account, as my case has been something singular; for in all my literary attempts I have been obliged to strike out my own path, by the light I could acquire from books, as I have not had a teacher or assistant since I was ten years of age.

One word concerning my views to the ministry, and I have done. I have told you, that this was my dear mother's hope concerning me, but her death, and the scenes in which I afterwards engaged, seemed to cut off the probability. The first desires in my own mind, arose many years ago, from a reflection on Gal. 2: 23-24: 'But they had heard only, that he which persecuted us in times past, now preacheth the faith which once he destroyed.' – which, as my life had been full of remarkable turns, and I seemed selected to show what the Lord could do, I was in some hopes that, perhaps, sooner or later, he might call me into this service, and this, I think, determined me to study the original Scriptures.

But the ministry remained an imperfect desire in my breast till it was recommended to me by some Christian friends. I started when the thought was first seriously proposed to me; but afterwards set apart some weeks to consider the case, to consult my friends, and to entreat the Lord's direction, all of which tended to engage me. My first thought was to join the Dissenters, from a presumption that I could not honestly make the required subscriptions, but Mr C—, in a conversation upon these points, moderated my scruples, and preferring the Established Church in some other respects, I accepted a title from him some months afterwards, and solicited ordination from the late Archbishop of York. I need not tell you I met a refusal, nor what steps I took afterwards to succeed elsewhere. At present I desist from applications. My desire to serve the Lord is not weakened, but I am not so hasty to push myself forward as I was formerly. It is sufficient that he will know how to dispose of me, and that he both can, and will, do what is best. To him I commend myself: I trust that his will and my true interest are inseparable. To his name be glory for ever. And thus I conclude my story, and presume you will acknowledge I have been particular enough. I have room for no more, but to repeat that,

I am, etc.

2 February 1763

Appendix: 'Amazing Grace'

The following is the text of the hymn now known as 'Amazing Grace', written by John Newton and first published as hymn XLI, Faith's Review and Expectation (1 Chronicles 17:16-17) in *Olney Hymns* (1779).

Amazing grace! (how sweet the sound!)
    That sav'd a wretch like me!
I once was lost, but now am found,
    Was blind, but now I see.

'Twas grace that taught my heart to fear,
    And grace my fears reliev'd;
How precious did that grace appear,
    The hour I first believ'd!

Through many dangers, toils, and snares,
    I have already come;
'Tis grace hath brought me safe thus far,
    And grace will lead me home.

The Lord has promis'd good to me,
   His word my hope secures;
He will my shield and portion be,
   As long as life endures.

Yes, when this flesh and heart shall fail,
   And mortal life shall cease:
I shall possess, within the veil,
   A life of joy and peace.

The earth shall soon dissolve like snow,
   The sun forbear to shine;
But God, who call'd me here below,
   Will be for ever mine.

Notes

1. Hochschild, Adam, *Bury the Chains: The British Struggle to Abolish Slavery* (London: Pan Macmillan, 2005), pp.20-21.
2. Turner, Steve, *Amazing Grace* (Oxford, Lion: 2005), pp.102-5.
3. Martin, Bernard, *John Newton and the Slave Trade* (London: Longman, 1961), p.55.
4. Hochschild, p.21.
5. Turner, p.73.
6. Walvin, James, *The Slave Trade* (Stroud: Sutton, 1999), x-xi.
7. Ibid., xiv, p.25.
8. Ibid., pp.15, 19.
9. See Rediker, Marcus, *The Slave Ship: A Human History* (London: John Murray, 2007), p.47, where he indicates that recent research suggests that the trade was not always truly triangular, as many slave ships found it difficult to source a return cargo for the journey home.
10. Hochschild, p.20.
11. Turner, pp.89, 90, 100.
12. Williamson, J G, 'The Structure of Pay in Britain, 1710-1911', *Research in Economic History*, 7 (1982), 1-54.
13. Aitken, Jonathan, *John Newton: From Disgrace to Amazing Grace* (London: Continuum, 2007), p.247. A first-hand account of the slave trade from the point of view of a surgeon on a slave trader was published by Alexander Falconbridge, entitled *An Account of the Slave Trade* (London: Phillips, 1788). Falconbridge accompanied Thomas Clarkson (1760-1836), the abolitionist, on his investigations into the trade and provided evidence for Clarkson's antislavery publications.
14. Rediker, pp.223-4.
15. Walvin, pp.24, 27.
16. Rediker, pp.49-50.
17. Ibid., p.50.
18. Aitken, pp.133-4.
19. See also, for example, Martin, p.67.

SEAFARERS' VOICES

A new series of seafaring memoirs

The lives and practices of our seafaring forebears have receded into the distant past, remote but also of fascination to a generation to whom the sea is now an alien place. This new series, Seafarers' Voices, presents a set of abridged and highly readable first-hand accounts of maritime voyaging, which describe life at sea from different viewpoints – naval, mercantile, officer and lower deck, men and women – and cover the years 1700 to the 1900s, from the end of the Mediterranean galleys, through the classic age of sail to the coming of the steamship. Published in chronological order, these memoirs unveil the extraordinary and unfamiliar world of our seafaring ancestors and show how they adapted to the ever-demanding and ever-changing world of ships and the sea, both at war and at peace.

The first titles in the series

1. *Galley Slave*, by Jean Marteilhe

2. *A Privateer's Voyage Round the World*, by Captain George Shelvocke

3. *Slaver Captain*, John Newton

4. *Landsman Hay*, Robert Hay

For more details visit our website
www.seaforthpublishing.com